CONTENTS

LIST OF FIGURES

PREFACE

The Internet has forever changed reference service by exponentially expanding the universe of available information. Now librarians are able to answer questions in almost any imaginable subject area. Internet technology introduces both challenges and opportunities to all aspects of librarianship, particularly in the reference arena. Librarians feel frustrated with determining which sites are the best for the question at hand. *Using the Internet as a Reference Tool: A How-To-Do-It Manual for Librarians* will teach you how to access, evaluate, and navigate Internet sites with the speed, efficiency, and comfort level we have long enjoyed with print sources.

The computer revolution in libraries over the last ten years has been amazing. As librarians master the challenges of the Internet, everyone is eager to learn new ways to answer the great variety of reference questions combining trusted sources with the new power of the Internet. There seems little argument that requests to use the Internet at reference desks are on the rise. Even librarians who initially found the Internet to be more of a waste of time than a useful tool now acknowledge that learning to use it cannot be avoided. Patrons often tell librarians that "I have to find this on the Internet." In many cases the request is more want than need, but many teachers are starting to require students to cite Internet sources in their research papers.

"Don't all reference desks use the Internet? Do librarians still need Internet training? Don't they all know it by now?" As an Internet trainer covering a twelve-state region, I answer that the ever-changing nature of the Internet requires "continuing education" in a way that our profession has never before demanded. While librarians are always eager to learn ways to do their job better and to provide the best reference service possible for their patrons, the Internet forces us to expand our skills and knowledge on an almost daily basis.

Offering a field-tested step-by-step workshop, *Using the Internet as a Reference Tool: A How-To-Do-It Manual for Librarians* will increase your skills and confidence in using the Internet in day-to-day reference situations. It is based on one of my most popular classes where I walk reference librarians through the steps necessary to use the Internet as efficiently as they do their print collection. By turning that class into this book, I hope to reach more librarians that need this information on how to best use the Internet. I want to make this incredible tool a successful part of every reference resource toolbox.

The audience for *Using the Internet as a Reference Tool: A How-To-Do-It Manual for Librarians* includes all types of librarians who put in hours at a reference desk answering patrons' questions. Students of MLS programs will also benefit from this book by using it as a textbook for what they need to prepare for that first day on an actual reference desk. This book is not limited in scope to any particular type of librarian (public, K–12, university, etc.) or subject area. Nor is this book limited to librarians in a particular locality or country. Even though most of my examples are based on sites in the United States and the United Kingdom, they use situations that are encountered by librarians the world over. If you work at a reference desk of any type, in any capacity, in any location, this book is for you.

After reading this book and doing the exercises, you will gain a number of skills necessary to successfully use the Internet in your search for answers to reference questions. You will learn the best way to evaluate both print and electronic resources, how to examine specific elements of a Web site, learn about bookmarks and how to create a Web-based reference page for your library. You will examine the differences between search engines and directories, and how to use the Internet when creating effective ready reference and complex reference strategies. With these skills in hand, you'll be able to utilize the Internet as effectively as you do your print resources in your day-to-day reference work. Please read the chapters in the order presented the first time through. After that, feel free to refer to individual sections as necessary.

Chapter 1, "Assessing the Impact of the Internet on Reference Services" discusses how the Internet is changing the way that reference service is delivered today. It explores ways that print can fail and how the Internet can help.

Chapter 2, "Evaluating Internet-Based Reference Resources" shows you how to determine whether a reference resource is appropriate for use in answering a question. The chapter discusses how to evaluate and compare print and Internet resources. Reference questions actually asked in library settings are utilized as the basis for informative (and often entertaining) hands-on evaluation exercises. These exercises provide experience in recognizing potentially incorrect or misleading information.

Chapter 3, "Creating An Effective Ready Reference Strategy" takes you through the process most librarians use when deciding whether to use print or the Internet to answer a ready reference question. Because we learned reference using a print model, this common process has some pitfalls. Chapter 3 reveals the problems associated with that process and offers an alternative decision-making strategy as well as the steps necessary to successfully implement it. It examines bookmarks and explores Web-based reference desk innovations. The chapter concludes with some real-life reference questions and Web sites you can use to practice this new strategy.

Chapter 4, "Comparing Search Engines and Directories" discusses the often hidden differences between a search engine and a directory. Once you learn the key similarities and differences between these two types of resources, you will be able to choose the right resource for each question. Chapter 4 explores different types of search engines and directories as well as how subject specific resources fill the gap when these more commonly used resources fail.

Chapter 5, "Creating a Complex Reference Strategy" shows you how to employ the Internet to answer questions that are more complex or involved than ready reference questions. It begins with an evaluation of your current print and Internet strategies and shows you how to create a new and effective Internet strategy. Real-life complex reference questions and Web searches and evaluation provide an opportunity for you to hone your skills.

Chapter 6, "Exploring Larger Issues of Internet Reference" looks at ways the Internet has changed the nature of reference services in libraries. It offers some "views from the front lines" of librarians as they offer assessments of e-mail reference services. This chapter concludes with a brief look at how the Internet may provide competition to traditional library reference.

The appendices, which list ready reference meta pages and online vertical files, supplement the extensive resources presented at the end of the individual chapters. Be sure to visit *www.neal-schuman.com/sauers/* the companion Web site for this book. You will find links to all of the resources listed in this book along with additional resources on all of the topics discussed. Periodically I will also be adding additional reference resources so be sure to check back every so often.

After taking my workshop, I'm happy to report that librarians report a new ease, expertise, and excitement using the Internet. My hope is that *Using the Internet as a Reference Tool: A How-To-Do-It Manual for Librarians* will help create a sense of empowerment, improve your abilities as a reference librarian, and help you offer your users the benefits of your skills.

ACKNOWLEDGMENTS

Many people, institutions, and technologies made this book possible. Most specifically I would like to express my appreciation and love for my wife Denice Adkins. Without her trust and support throughout this project I would not get all this writing done at all, let alone on time. Her research assistance was also an integral part of the genesis of this book and it would not be nearly as good as it is without her.

I would also like to thank Jennifer, Delilah, and Jeff at the Starbucks on the corner of Mississippi and Havana in Aurora, Colorado for their nonfat white chocolate mochas, United Airlines for their delays, DEN and CHI for the uncomfortable seats in which I was able to get much of this work completed, Laura for her editing skills, MP3 technology for allowing me to listen to all the music I wanted to without making the CD player suck all the battery life out of my laptop, Charles "what's-his-name" Harmon (inside joke) of Neal-Schuman for having the faith in this idea in the first place, Dr. Bill Katz for introducing me to the wonderful world of reference service, all of my co-workers at BCR for making sure my head never grows too large, all of the librarians and library staff that have attended all of my workshops over the years, and all the members on the online library community that supplied me with the stories I quoted throughout this book. Thanks also to the people who granted me permission to use their Web sites in the evaluation exercises. You can find a complete list in the "Notes & Credits" section on page 133. Lastly I would like to thank the members of the Dean Koontz E-mailers (available at: *homepage @ www.webpan.com/msauers/koontz/faq.html*) for all their encouragement for my writing projects however unrelated to them it may be.

1 ASSESSING THE IMPACT OF THE INTERNET ON REFERENCE SERVICES

HOW THE INTERNET CHANGES REFERENCE SERVICES

To deny that the Internet has had a major impact on libraries' reference services to their patrons would be the equivalent of denying that the sun rises in the east and sets in the west. The Internet has changed reference services in both positive and negative ways.

Some of the more obvious positive ways are:

- More up-to-date information can be found.
- Information can be found more quickly.
- "The Internet has given us access to resources, such as government publications, that we could not have provided in any other way." [Dorothy Fleishman, librarian at an unnamed medium-sized public library]

A positive but less obvious way is that:

- "many more requests for information are coming via e-mail. In most cases it is easier for me to respond to these via e-mail than through other traditional methods." [Jim Pate, Birmingham (AL) Public Library]

A few negative ways the Internet has affected reference services are:

- False or misleading information is more common online than in print.
- Many users are going to the Internet as a replacement for the library reference desk.
- The sheer number of results found can easily confuse novice users.

> Academic reference librarians responding to a survey indicated that their job satisfaction increased as the number of electronic reference resources increased. Many respondents indicated that teaching became a larger part of their role as reference librarians, as library patrons indicated the need for more guidance.
>
> Source: Carol Tenopir. "The Impact of Digital Reference on Librarians and Library Users." *Online* 22(6): November 1998. pp. 84+.

- "People from all over ask us questions that our collection can handle." [Steve Garwood, Camden (NJ) Public Library]

Using the Internet as a Reference Tool will help you confront issues dealing with these changes.

HOW PRINT RESOURCES CAN FAIL

Print resources have been around longer than libraries and are not going away any time soon. Print will continue to be the central part of library reference collections for the foreseeable future. However, print reference collections do have significant limitations that we must acknowledge and accept.

- Print reference resources are out-of-date the moment they are published. The lead time on the average book today is three to six months and that is just from completion of the manuscript to publication. Add to this the time that it takes for the data to be collected and organized, and the

> "It is reasonable to assume that an experienced searcher's efforts will result in success that at least equals the success of the majority of users of the Internet."
>
> Source: Tschera Harkness Connell and Jennifer E. Tipple. "Testing the Accuracy of Information on the World Wide Web using the AltaVista Search Engine." *Reference & User Services Quarterly*, 38(4): Summer 1999. pp. 360+.

material in the book may be more than a year old by the time it's published.

- Print reference resources are not searchable. Good indexing can help, but full-text searching is just not possible in a print resource.
- Print reference resources are not very portable. Yes, you can physically move a book around easily, but what percentage of your reference collection cannot be removed from the library? Ninety percent? One hundred percent? Is this portable?
- Print reference resources are not accessible to more than one person at a time. This limits the quick and easy accessibility of the material. A line of patrons waiting to use the blue book is not good reference service.

HOW THE INTERNET CAN HELP

I am not one of those people who claim the Internet is an end-all be-all solution to all life's problems (nor even to all questions that you will receive at the reference desk). I will, however, claim that it can provide potential solutions to the problems we face with print resources. For example:

- Internet resources are accessible from any connected computer. Subject to licensing agreements that your library may have with a vendor, a Web page can be accessed by any computer connected to the Internet from any location. This allows patrons to access the material at their convenience.

One site, for instance, allows you to search a database of acronyms and abbreviations. Type in *SCUBA* and get back Self Contained Underwater Breathing Apparatus. Yes, you can also get that in a print acronym dictionary, but this same site will also search for results that contain what you searched on as a subset. As shown in Figure 1–1, a search on *ala* not only finds the acronym ALA but also AAALAC, AALAS, ALANON, and others.

- Internet resources can be more current. Internet publishing is nearly instantaneous. This removes the three- to six-month delay that print resources must have to produce the physical object.

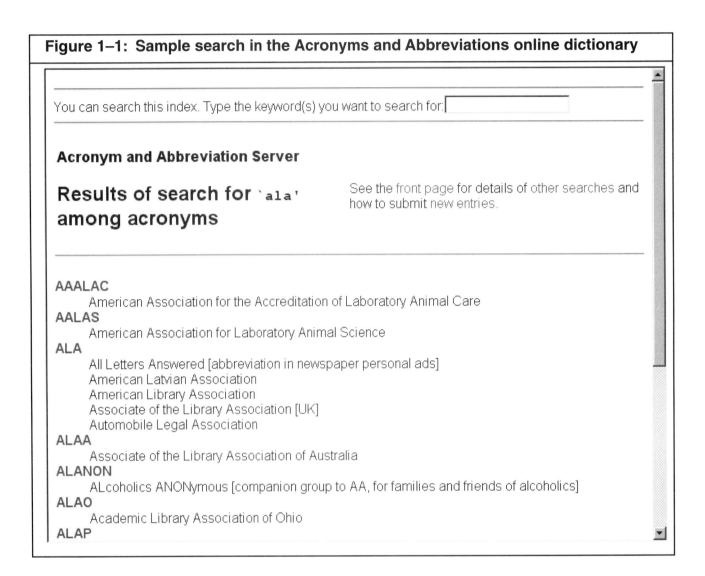

Figure 1–1: Sample search in the Acronyms and Abbreviations online dictionary

You can search this index. Type the keyword(s) you want to search for:

Acronym and Abbreviation Server

Results of search for 'ala' among acronyms

See the front page for details of other searches and how to submit new entries.

AAALAC
American Association for the Accreditation of Laboratory Animal Care
AALAS
American Association for Laboratory Animal Science
ALA
All Letters Answered [abbreviation in newspaper personal ads]
American Latvian Association
American Library Association
Associate of the Library Association [UK]
Automobile Legal Association
ALAA
Associate of the Library Association of Australia
ALANON
ALcoholics ANONymous [companion group to AA, for families and friends of alcoholics]
ALAO
Academic Library Association of Ohio
ALAP

- Many people can access Internet resources at the same time. Subject to licensing agreements, one person or one thousand people can access a particular Web page at any time, thus eliminating, or at least reducing, those lines in the library for limited physical resources.

Figure 1–2: Date disclaimer in the CIA World Factbook online

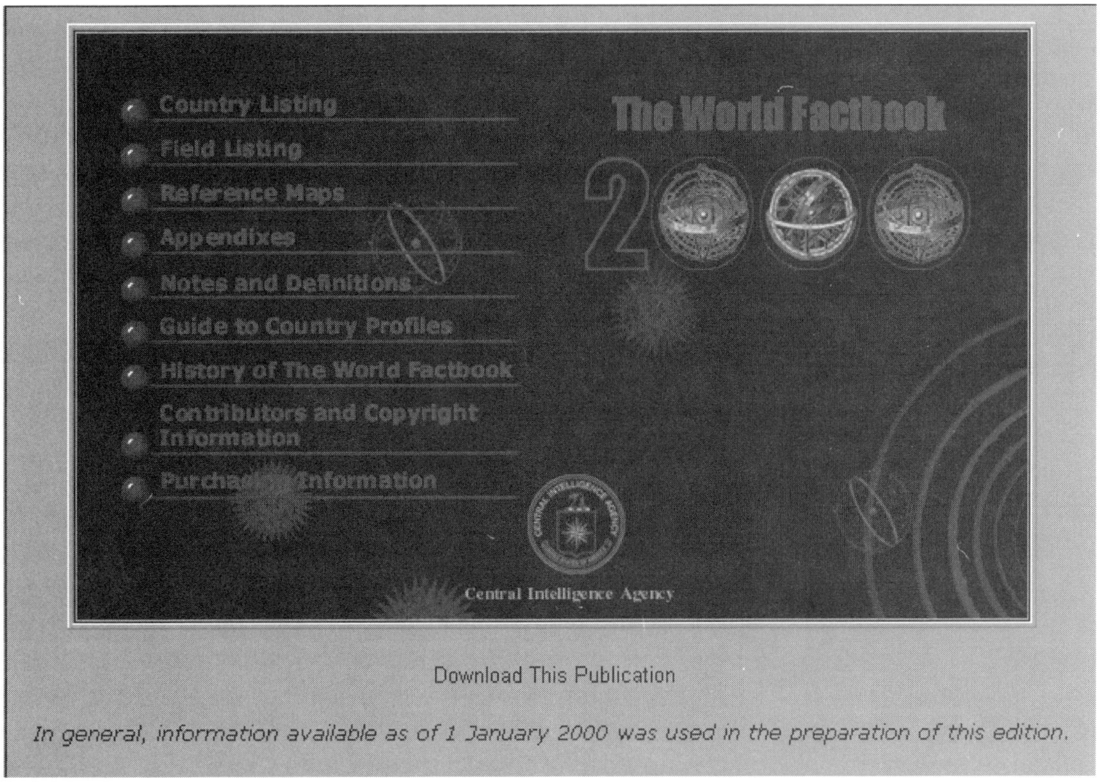

Country Listing

Field Listing

Reference Maps

Appendixes

Notes and Definitions

Guide to Country Profiles

History of The World Factbook

Contributors and Copyright Information

Purchasing Information

The World Factbook 2000

Central Intelligence Agency

Download This Publication

In general, information available as of 1 January 2000 was used in the preparation of this edition.

HOW THE INTERNET STILL NEEDS TO GROW

As I have said before, I am not one of those people who think print is dead and the Internet is our salvation. The Internet faces many challenges.

- Connections cost money. Please notice that I said "connections," not sites. (We'll deal with site costs in the Evaluation section.) Equipment costs money, the connection itself costs money, some even tell me that staff time costs money (though hopefully we'll reduce that one as a result of this book).
- Just because it is online doesn't mean it is more up-to-date. This is an assumption that many people make, including librarians. People assume that if the information

"When asked how they would answer a general fact-based question, 32% of respondents to a 1998 survey said they would consult a print source first, and 22% recommended consulting an electronic source like the Internet or paid subscription databases. However, an impressive 46% said that it depends!"

Source: Mark Stover. "Reference Librarians and the Internet: A Qualitative Study." *Reference Services Review* 28(1), 2000. pp. 39–46.

is online it must be current as of yesterday. This is a misconception that must be corrected. For example, the CIA World Factbook online is no more current than the print version. It is not kept up-to-date based on the day's world events. I recently checked the site (see Figure 1–2) and it said on the front page "in general, information available as of 1 January 2000 was used in the preparation of this edition." In other words, the majority of material in this Internet resource is out-of-date. They state it up front, but many users overlook the disclaimer.

- The size of the Internet is always mentioned as a major problem to users. At the end of the year 2000, there were estimated to be more than two billion pages on the Internet, more than double the 1999 figure. Although they are not all findable (we'll discuss this later), that is a large collection of information. Add to this the statistic that there are three new pages appearing on the Internet every second and you can just imagine how fast this collection is growing.

- Quality of information is also a big problem. One maxim that I believe in when dealing with the Internet is that the best thing about the Internet is that anyone can publish whatever he or she wants. The trouble is that the worst thing about the Internet is also that anyone can publish whatever he or she wants.

2 EVALUATING INTERNET-BASED REFERENCE RESOURCES

Almost every time I have attended or addressed a gathering of more than a dozen librarians, someone has brought up the issue of evaluating Internet resources. It doesn't matter whether it's a small informal gathering or a national level conference—someone asks about or discusses the evaluation of Web sites. A quick search of library literature from 1998 through late 2000 finds more than 200 published articles on the topic. Although there is much debate, you would think all this research has helped librarians know how to decide whether a Web site is any good. You may not realize how much you know already.

If there is one thing I have learned from all of the classes that I have taught, it is to start with what the students know. I am going to make an assumption here—that you are familiar with print resources. You have used them, you have selected them, and you have purchased them. Regardless of the purpose—whether for business or for pleasure—before using, before selecting, and before purchasing, you have first evaluated that resource.

Sometimes the evaluation process is simple: you scan the copy of the dust jacket flaps to decide if, let's say, this new mystery would be something your patron would like to read. Sometimes it's a complex process; for example, you need to find the best reference resource for a PhD student on a particular topic for a dissertation.

Now, ask yourself this: what are the most important things to consider when evaluating a print resource to add to your reference collection?

EVALUATING PRINT RESOURCES

A librarian should consider the following six items when evaluating a work for inclusion in a reference collection. These items are not in any particular order of importance; the importance of each item will depend on the work: its subject and the numerous other variables of each particular situation.

In a survey of librarians who use the Internet, 63% of respondents felt their patrons weren't able to determine whether information from the Internet was authoritative. Teaching patrons how to evaluate Internet resources was indicated as a "legitimate professional responsibility."

Source: Stover, Mark. "Reference Librarians and the Internet: A Qualitative Study." *Reference Services Review* 28(1), 2000. pp. 39-46.

1. **Purpose**

   The purpose of a reference work should be evident from the title or form. The two purposes you generally have to pick from are information and persuasion. Since we are talking about a reference collection, you should be able to rule out anything in which the purpose is persuasion. Those works fit better in the general nonfiction collection. Once you have determined that the purpose of the work is to provide information, you must then ask yourself whether the author or compiler has fulfilled that purpose. If the title of the work is *A Complete Guide to Chess* and you know something about chess, try looking up some information in the work. If someone with a layperson's knowledge of the subject can easily notice missing information, the work is not complete and therefore does not live up to its purpose.

2. **Authority**

   As the evaluator of the work you must ask yourself the following questions about the author and/or publisher of the work: What are the author's qualifications in regard to the subject? Is the author a layperson with significant knowledge of the subject or does he or she hold a PhD in that area? Does the author's background predispose him or her to any bias on the topic? Politically sensitive topics such as race and reproduction are areas that need to be carefully considered. Does the publisher or the imprint signify the quality of the work? Some publishers are known for publishing significant previous works on certain topics and can be expected to continue to do so. If the publisher is a new one, its reputation will not have been established and additional scrutiny may be called for.

3. **Scope**

   Most often when I am quizzing the attendees of this work-shop, someone brings up "currency" as an item for consideration. What they mean is that the book should be up-to-date. In most cases you will be looking for the most current version of a reference book, but not necessarily.

   For example, I have a book published by the Rand Corporation titled *A Million Random Digits with 100,000 Normal Deviates*. Despite its having been published in 1955, I have no need to purchase a newer edition. If I need a random number this book works just as well as it did the day it was published.

   This item is better termed "scope"—Does the book cover information that other works in the collection do not? In most cases this may be determined based on the fact that the work is the most current on the topic and therefore covers more material than previous editions. In some cases however, an older work may cover an aspect of a subject that a newer work does not. In this case the work may be appropriate in scope despite its not being the most current. Scope does not need to be limited to time frame. You can also view scope from the angles of geography and subject content.

4. **Audience**

   Whenever you consider adding a new work to your collection you must keep in mind who your audience is and what they want or need. Who makes up your audience is more apparent than what they need. A university reference collection will include different material than will a public library's collection. Within a public library, the adult reference collection will be significantly different from the children's reference collection. These determinations can be easily made based on the age and education levels of the library's patrons.

   Determining what each group wants or needs may not be as easy at first, but you must try to do it all the time. The patrons of a university library will ask, in most cases, significantly more complex and detailed questions than will the patrons of a public library because the need is different. You also must consider what the patrons want. Although this may seem similar to need at first, the differences between want and need are significant. In some cases you may end up adding works to your collection due to patron demand for a new popular work, despite the fact that you may have a better or more complete work already in the collection. Remember, we are here to serve our patrons.

5. **Format**

   Format can also be thought of in two different ways: the usability of the work and the physical size of the work.

   The usability of the work is usually the overriding consideration of the two. Does the work have an index? Is it organized chronologically or alphabetically? Ultimately, can users find the information they are looking for in the work without too much hassle? The answer you are looking for is Yes. If the work is too cumbersome for your average patron, then it is probably not a useful edition to your reference collection.

   Physical size of the work is not always considered since most works are of a traditional size. But what about a complete set of the *Oxford English Dictionary*? The complete set is 20 volumes and easily takes up one whole shelf. For a small library with limited shelf space, this can be an overriding consideration in whether to add this work to the collection. Instead, the small library may decide to go with the compact, two-volume edition (though that has its own set of problems due to print so small it comes with its own magnifying glass) or an abridged edition.

6. **Cost**

   I never like bringing this one up but it must get a mention. All of the other five items in this list usually end up being thrown out as irrelevant if the work you want does not fit into your budget.

As I mentioned before the list, these items are not presented in a particular order. In one case cost might be the most important; in another, audience might be. Let me give you a few scenarios where one may be more important than another.

- A small public library thinks that it would like to add the *Oxford English Dictionary* to their collection. The librarian knows that the dictionary will take up a lot of space but feels that she can make the room for it. She quickly realizes that shelf room is irrelevant when she finds that the complete set will cost somewhere in the neighborhood of $2,000. In comparison, the very small print of the compact edition seems an acceptable compromise for the much lower price of about $200.

> What do you mean when you say "Internet resource"? These days, you can equate an Internet resource to a Web site. However, all Web sites are not created equal. What should not be included in this discussion are services like Lexis-Nexis and OCLC's FirstSearch. These online databases charge user fees outside the price range of an individual home user. Although you can use the Internet to access them, for the purposes of this book I do not consider them Internet resources because they were around before the Internet as we know it today, they have just evolved to fit the Internet model, and they are not readily accessible by your patrons without your library's direct involvement in supplying access to those resources. A service such as netLibrary is considered an Internet resource since it started purely as an Internet-based service and it is accessible directly to patrons without your library's involvement.

- The library at a university with a brand-new physics department, at first, may not have the amount of quality reference material that it will need to support the department. In this situation cost may need to be completely overlooked for one budgetary cycle in order to build up that area of the collection to the necessary level.
- A new book is published on a current hot topic or recommended on television and generates great demand. Though the scope of the book may not cover the material in the detail that the librarian may like, the book would be purchased because of public demand. Had the demand not existed, another title on the same topic may have been purchased.

EVALUATING INTERNET RESOURCES

Now that we have looked at what you already knew about—print resources—let's move along to what you're here to learn; evaluating Internet resources.

What do you need to look at when evaluating an Internet resource? Have you considered purpose, authority, scope, audience, cost, and format? Do those six items sound familiar? They should. They are the same six items we considered when evaluating a print resource, though we do need to consider some of them in a slightly different way.

- **Purpose**
  This criterion does not vary much from its print counterpart. What is the purpose of the work and has the author fulfilled that purpose? Is the purpose to inform or persuade? If the purpose of the site is to sell you something, that may not automatically invalidate the information but it must be considered. (I'll cover this in much more detail later in the book.)

- **Authority**
  This can be considered in the same manner as print—What are the qualifications of the author? You do, however, need to give a little more scrutiny when it comes to the Internet. With print, one can usually assume an author must have a minimal amount of authority on a topic before a publisher will accept his or her work for publication. With the Internet this is definitely not the case. I always like to ask my students the following two questions: What is the best thing about the Internet? What is the worst? The answer is the same for both questions: Anyone can publish whatever they want with little effort or expense. This is the central paradox to the power of the Internet.

- **Scope**
  Does the site cover a time or topic better than print resources? Many people believe that since something is on the Internet it will automatically be more up-to-date than any print counterpart. This is not always the case and therefore a poor assumption to make. (I will discuss this further later in the book.)

- **Audience**
  Although there is no real difference between Internet and print on this item, the question is much more controversial when it comes to the Internet. If this were not a concern, filtering in libraries would not be the prominent issue librarians face every day.

- **Cost**
  This has always been a difficult one for me. One month, I agree with those who say cost is an issue, the next I disagree. Before I go any further in explaining myself, let me establish one point: I am not considering sites such as Lexis-Nexis, OCLC's FirstSearch, and many other online databases. Yes, you must pay for access to these services, but the Internet is just the delivery method. I do not consider

"Two Colorado librarians wanted to learn 'what kind of practical reference bang a library gets from its Internet buck.' Without using subscription databases or online encyclopedias, they found answers to 61% of their 209 patron-generated questions! In terms of reference services, they concluded that the Internet was worth the investment, and might benefit smaller libraries even more than it would benefit larger libraries with more extensive reference collections."

Source: Joseph R. Zumalt and Robert W. Pasicznyuk. "The Internet and Reference Services." *Reference and User Services Quarterly* 38(2): Winter 1998. pp. 165+.

these "Internet resources" for the purposes of this book. That being said, is cost still an issue?

Librarians who believe that cost *is* an issue generally make the following points: The Internet costs money in access fees, equipment, and staff time. On the surface, these are valid arguments.

The counterargument to this is that these concerns are like trying to factor in the cost of the shelf that a book will sit on into the decision whether to buy the book. These are capital costs and fall under the cost of doing business. Once you have paid for the equipment and the connection, cost should not be considered when evaluating a particular site. As for staff time, dealing with print resources takes up staff time, too. Maybe not as much, but time nonetheless.

Consider, however, that there are Web sites out there that cost money to use, usually as a per-use fee. One example is the special collection area of Northern Light. The site allows the user to perform a search for full-text articles. The citations for and brief summaries of the articles are free. However, if you want the article itself, you must

In my search engines class I recommend that even though you may know that neither you (the library) nor the patron are willing to pay the fee, you should not avoid searching the special collection area of Northern Light. If you find a relevant article, the summary may answer your question and if it does not, you will still have a citation that may allow you to get the article from another database, such as OCLC's FirstSearch, which the library already pays for.

An article in the *Journal of the American Medical Association* discusses rating instruments that serve to identify health information on the Web. The researcher found 47 different rating instruments for health-related Web sites; however, only 14 of those instruments made their rating criteria available! The author writes, "It is unclear . . . whether [these ratings instruments] lead to more good than harm."

Source: Alejandro R. Jadad. "Rating Health Information on the Internet: Navigating to Knowledge or Babel?" *Journal of the American Medical Association* 279(9): February 25, 1998. pp. 611–614.

pay a fee for that article ranging from approximately $1.00 to $4.00. This is a site that is free to access and use, but may end up costing you some money for the information itself. In this case, cost is an issue.

As an example, I had a person looking for the date on which Desmond Llewellen (Q in the James Bond films) died. In a search of the special collections area of Northern Light I was able to find the obituary from the *London Times*. The citation listed the date of the article and the summary stated, "died yesterday." Using only the citation and a little math, we had the answer.

- **Format**
Format is much more interesting when it comes to an Internet resource than it is with print. In print, whether a book has an index and how the book is organized can be quickly and easily established. With an Internet resource there is much more to consider. Is there a search feature? How is the site organized? Can the site be easily navigated? Is the screen readable? Is the document printable? Let's take a look at these and other questions in more detail.

EXAMINING SPECIFIC ITEMS ON A WEB SITE

When evaluating a print resource many librarians are quick to flip to the copyright page to find information such as date published, publisher name, or other useful data. On the other hand, when we get to a Web site there is usually no copyright page to go to, or even, in more cases than I wish to count, any clear indication of who wrote the page or when. So, what can we look for or look at to help us find the information we need to successfully evaluate an Internet resource?

- **URL (Uniform Resource Locator)**
  A URL is the address used to specify the location of a resource that is available electronically. The trouble with using URLs is that they can be very misleading. For example, what does the tilde (~) mean to you? You probably answered that it means this document is a "personal page," that is, a page not necessarily representing the views of a larger organization, such as a company. This is no longer always true. Take a look at these three examples:

  1. *www.bcr.org/~msauers/classrooms.html*
  2. *www.webpan.com/msauers/Modesitt/*
  3. *www.bcr.org/~ids/Reference/*

The first example is a personal page in the classic definition. The text following the ~ is a *username*; this is my personal page at the BCR Web site (my employer) and is not officially part of the BCR site. It is just an area of the BCR Web server in which I am allowed some freedom to do what I will.

The second example is a personal page despite the non-appearance of a tilde. This is my non-work-related Web site hosted on the server of an ISP (Internet service provider) that has decided not to use tildes. (They don't have to if they don't want to.)

The last is the URL of a Web page that is *not* a personal page; this Web page is officially part of the BCR site, even though a tilde does appear in the URL. When the BCR

In one of my classes I was told by a university reference librarian that one of the professors on campus had forbidden his students from citing in their assignments any Web page with a tilde in the URL since tildes indicated a "personal page" and therefore made the information suspect. Well, this *ruled out* most of BCR's site despite its authority and *ruled in* my personal pages even though I might not have authority. In this example, the professor would have automatically had his students include my personal page and exclude almost the complete BCR Web site, which is the opposite of what he intended.

Web server was set up, someone decided to divide up the server in a way that requires tildes to appear in the URLs. The point is, you cannot state for a fact that the appearance of a tilde makes a Web page a personal page, or that the lack of a tilde makes that page a non-personal page.

Another part of the URL people usually look at is the Top Level Domain (TLD). This is the last part of the domain name in a URL. Here's what the most common TLDs mean:

.COM
Commercial (for-profit) organizations in the United States. Anyone in the United States can register a .com domain.

.NET
Traditionally refers to Internet-related companies such as ISPs but is realistically available for almost anyone (in the United States).

.ORG
Not-for-profit organizations though open to almost anyone in the United States as long as they are not using the site for profit.

.EDU
Reserved for U.S. colleges and universities of two-year or higher degree levels.

.GOV
Originally reserved for the U.S. federal government but recently opened to U.S. municipalities.

.MIL
Reserved for the U.S. military.

Late in 2000, the Internet Corporation for Assigned Names and Numbers (ICANN) announced that it was considering seven new top-level domains. As of the publication of this book these domains had not been given final approval. They are .aero, .biz, .coop, .info, .museum, .name, and .pro.

.INT
International organizations such as the United Nations, NATO, and the European Union.

See any patterns here? With the exception of .INT (which is hardly ever used) all you can guarantee from many of them is that they are in the United States. Once you get out of the country you then encounter two-letter country codes (for example, .UK, .CA, .MX) under which each country has its own method of delineating between the different types of sites. (Many countries use .ac for academic sites, such as *www.oxford.ac.uk*.) K–12 schools and regional governments in the United States tend to use the .US domain preceded by a two-letter state code (for example, *www.state.co.us*.)

Some then like to argue that, well, .EDUs are more reliable than .COMs. I counter that this is a very dangerous assumption. Just as some .COMs have agendas and biases, so do some schools. Just because a .COM may be trying to ultimately sell you something does not mean that its information is suspect. (Though a healthy dose of skepticism never hurt anyone.)

How reliable the information out of a .GOV may or may not be is also up for debate depending on the topic and your personal political leanings.

- **Date**
Dates are always good things to look for on Web pages or sites. The most common date to appear is the date that a page was last updated. But is it accurate?

It is easy for the author of a page to make that (updated) date automatically display today's date without your knowing it. This way it seems as if the page is updated daily. This is not to say that all Web page authors are trying to deceive you but you need to keep this in mind.

In a less nefarious situation, suppose I create a page and manually type in the date at the bottom of the page (that

> Some Netscape users (depending on version) have the ability to type *about:document* into their location field to get additional information about a page. In most cases this information will include the "Last Modified" field, which reports the date on the file on the server, that is, when the file was last saved to the server. This date can be considered much more accurate than the date that appears on the page itself.

is how most authors do it). This means that whenever I update that page I must remember to update the date also. In many cases I might simply forget. I might have updated that page six times in the last two weeks, but have not updated the date in that time period. In this case, the date is wrong—but behind, not ahead as in the first example.

- **Contact information**
  Typically the contact information will be in the form of an e-mail address, since we are dealing with the Internet. But I like to suggest going further than that. Just because the site appears on the Internet, creators often forget to include a physical location. How about a phone number and a street address?

  Even libraries overlook this feature. I am still surprised at the number of library Web sites I have visited that do not list an address for the library. (I am not just picking on small publics.) I have needed to travel to major university libraries and wanted to go to MapQuest to get directions. First I need an address for the library to which I'll be traveling. I go to its Web site only to find no address whatsoever. I often end up calling the circulation desk to get an address. Do not assume that only local patrons are using your site and therefore already know where you are. Another point about contact information: I want to be able to contact the person or persons responsible for the content of the document, not just the person responsible for the site as a whole. Many times you'll find something like "Send comments to the Webmaster" in which the word "Webmaster" is an e-mail hyperlink. That's fine if the Webmaster is the one who wrote the document. This is

---

If a page you are on offers no navigational links through links on the page, do not panic. There may be another way that you can establish context by deconstructing the URL. Take that long URL in your browser's location field and start chopping off the end to single slashes. If you're at *www.somewhere.com/junk/stuff/other/ what.html* try *www.somewhere.com/junk/stuff/other/* or *www.somewhere.com/junk/stuff/* to see what you get. Keep chopping off the end until you get somewhere useful. Please be aware however, that when you do this you will receive your fair share of "404 - Not Found" errors since there may not be a page to be displayed at the new URL you have just created. Just ignore them and keep chopping; you will find something eventually.

Figure 2–1: Site search link on the BCR Web site

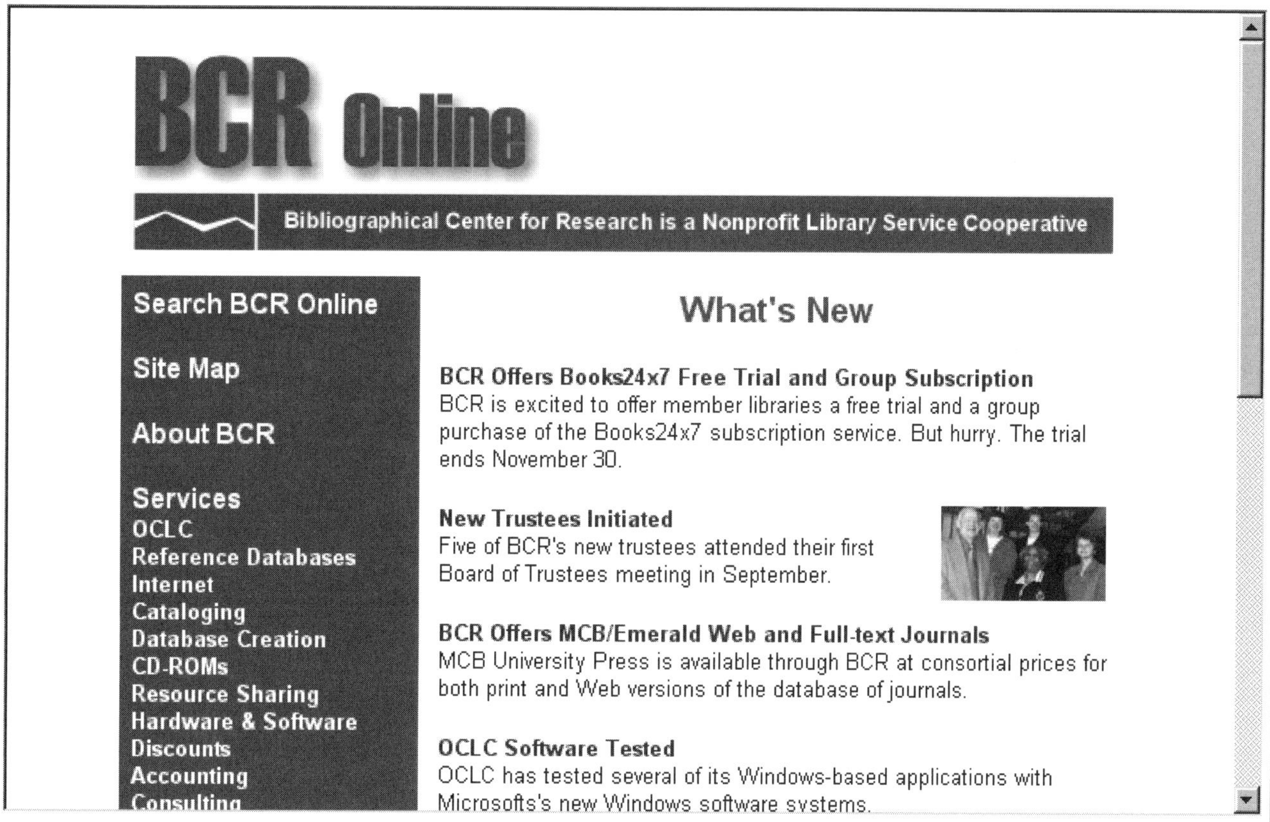

not fine if the Webmaster is the server administrator and stuck in some closet elsewhere on campus.

- **Home button for context**
Nothing is more frustrating than doing a search through some service like HotBot or AltaVista and ending up on a page six levels deep into a site. The search engine doesn't care about the context of that page at all. It just knows that the word or words you were looking for are on that page somewhere. A good site will consider this and offer you (at a minimum) a link to the site's homepage. This will allow you to establish the context that most isolated documents lack.

- **Overall site design**
Does the color scheme give you a headache just looking at it? When moving through a site can you tell that you are still in the same site, or do you have to keep looking up at the URL to be sure?

Figure 2–2: Author authority link on a personal Web site

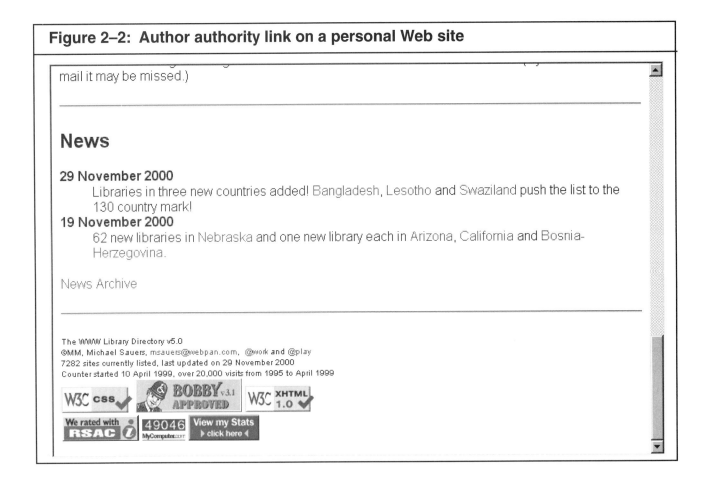

These and many other concerns are what you need to keep in mind when evaluating a site's design. Remember, you are probably considering whether to use this site again. If the site is obnoxious, regardless of the quality of information, you will not want to send your patrons there, or even return yourself.

- **Searchability**
  Something we always look at when evaluating a print resource is whether or not there is an index and, if so, whether it is any good. In the case of a Web site, the equivalent would be either a site search feature and/or a site map (see Figure 2–1). The appearance of these options, assuming they are easy to use, can be a significant enhancement to a larger site.

- **Link to a larger organization**
  Just because a site is hosted on an ISP instead of a company Web site does not mean that the author is not an

I have been using the Internet long enough that in most cases I have been able to just tune out advertisements that appear on Web pages. The ones that do bug me, however, are the ones that look like error messages. (There is a classic one out there that says "Warning, your connection is too slow" and it looks just like a MS Windows error message.) What bothers me about them is that they tend to make new Internet users more nervous about using the Internet than they already are. This is counter to the spirit of the Internet.

authority on the topic. For example, I have a personal site titled The World Wide Web Library Directory (see Figure 2–2). It is not hosted on the BCR Web site because it was a project I started before coming to BCR and something I plan on continuing if I ever leave. So, when someone comes to the site, they may wonder who the author is and why that author should be trusted to present such a resource. On that site is a link to BCR that establishes me as a BCR employee. By learning a little about BCR, the user should be able to determine my authority on the topic.

- **Load time**
One person's fast loading page is another person's slow loading page. There are many things that an author of a page can do to decrease the load time of a page, but it ultimately comes down to the speed of the user's Internet connection. A page that may load in 10 seconds on a T1 connection may take five times as long over a 28.8kbps modem.

What you, the user, must decide is whether the site's information is worth whatever wait you must endure to get to the information. If the site is the best available you might be willing to wait a little longer. If there is another site that is just as good, but loads in less time, then you may end up using that one instead.

- **Advertisements**
Advertisements bother some people and not others. My suggestion is to consider whether the advertisements detract from the information or are just a general annoyance.

In some cases, one of the central purposes of the site is to advertise a product or service. But does that fact necessarily invalidate the information? I would say no. Take the example of the Biography.com site (see Figure 2–3) run

Figure 2–3: Page header on the Biography.com site showing the link to the A&E Store

by the Arts & Entertainment cable network at *www. biography.com/*.

Take a few minutes to try this site out. It is a wonderful site for finding biographical information on thousands of famous and historical persons. All you need is a last name and you can get the basic biographical information and links to additional resources on the person you're looking for. A&E puts all of this up for your free use. Why do they do this? Because they would also like you to watch their network and purchase their videos. In fact, at the top of most of the sites pages is a link to their online store.

In this case, the whole site could be considered one giant advertisement for A&E. Should this fact cause you to think that the information is suspect? One might argue that this fact actually validates the information since A&E might lose viewers if they supplied incorrect information.

- **Graphics and Color**
Too many graphics or too few, depending on the site's topic, may influence your evaluation of a site. Too many graphics may also significantly affect load time of the page. Besides possibly giving you a headache if you look at it for too long, color scheme can also affect the printability of the document.

- **Printing**
This topic doesn't usually come up in my live workshops but should be considered in certain circumstances. If a site gives long answers to questions, you may need to print out the document and let the patron walk off with it. If the document does not print correctly, or needs additional steps on your part to make it print correctly (for example, changing the page orientation to landscape (see Figure 2–4), or setting Netscape to print all text in black), you might consider this an inefficient use of your time, thus causing

Figure 2–4: Sample document designed to be too wide to print in landscape mode

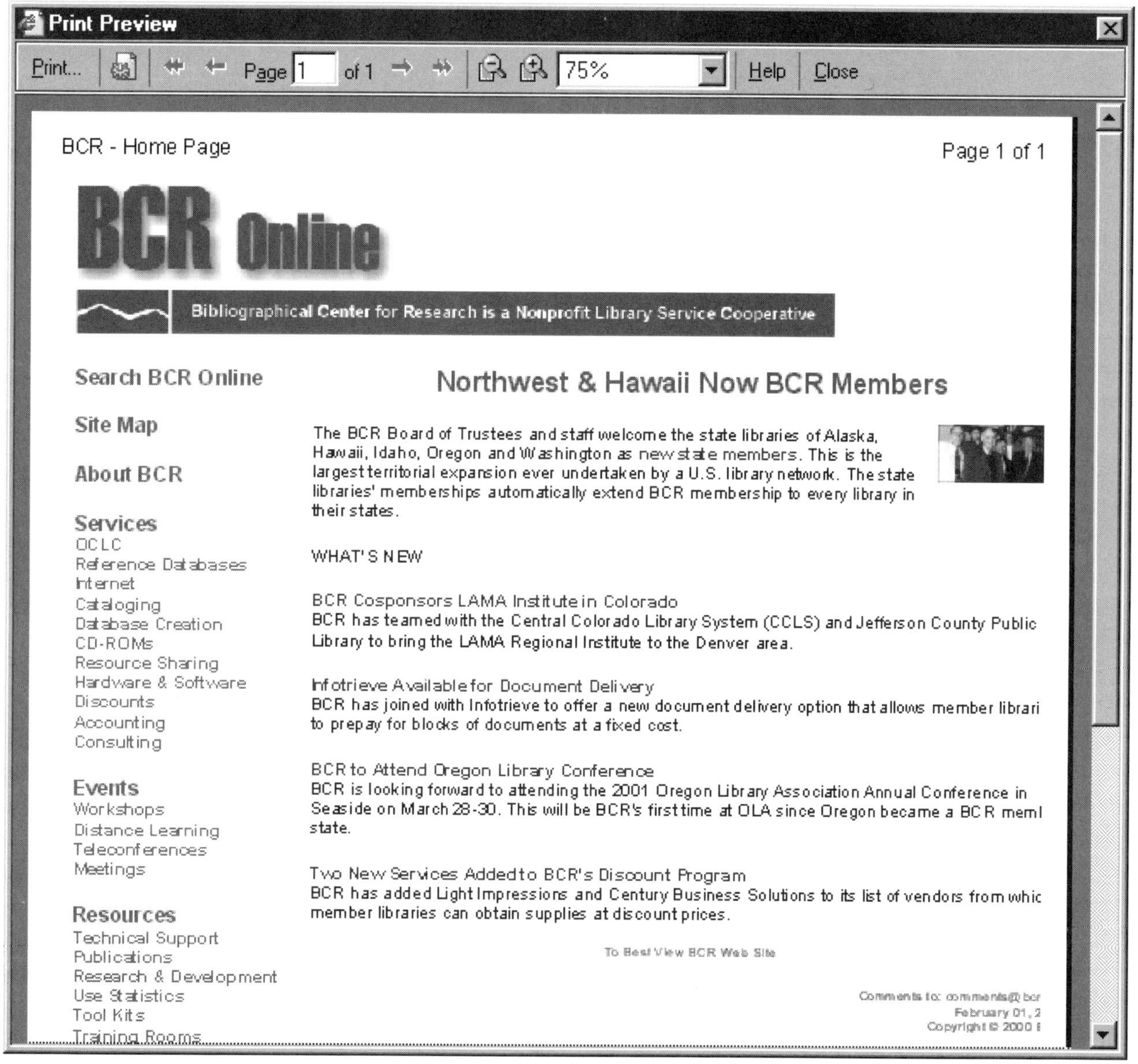

you to look for another resource that does not present these problems.

- **Hit Counters**
In previous years little counters at the bottom of pages were plentiful. Recently you may have noticed that they are not nearly as common as they used to be. Like a tilde in a URL, a stigma has been attached to the use of counters.

Figure 2–5: Web page with counter on the L. E. Modesitt, Jr., fan site

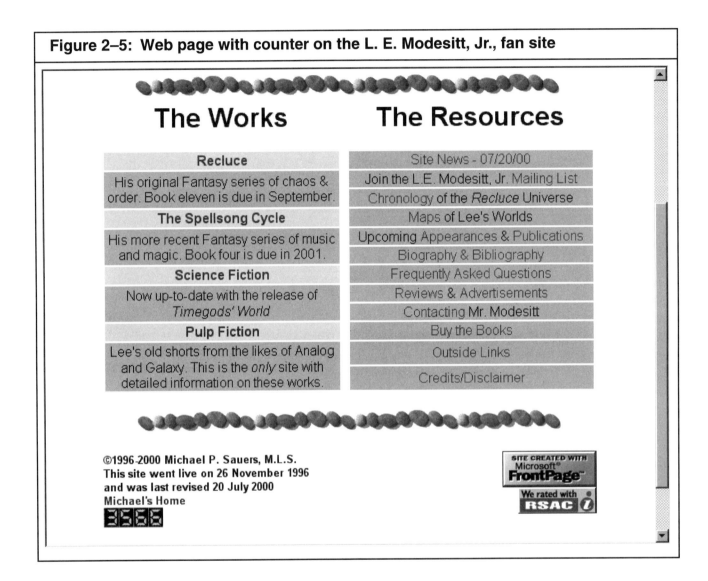

What a hit counter does is increment itself every time a user loads the page. This does not mean that the user hung around or was able to find what they were looking for, just that the user loaded the page. You might also question the number. It is technically possible to program a counter to increment by five (instead of one) whenever the page is loaded.

Since counters are unreliable, people who run professional Web sites now feel that their site's content should speak for itself and that they shouldn't have to prove how popular their site may or may not be through the use of a hit counter. The other reason for the decline in the use of

---

Figure 2–6: Awards Web page of the I80 Speedway

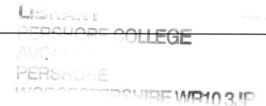

Home · Awards

Awards

Thank you to all that have graciously bestowed these awards upon us!

Event Schedule
Ticket Info
Directions
Top 10 Standings
Weekly Results
360 Sprints Standings
Pro Am Standings
Hobby Stock Standings
Late Model Standings
Modified Standings
I80 Speedway Messages Board
Hobby Stock Rules
Late Model Rules
Pro Am Rules
360 Sprints Rules
GPORRA Rules
Employment Opportunities
Racing Links
Awards we have won
Home

---

hit counters is that the visitor information is available through the server logs so the lack of a counter does not eliminate marketing information from a Webmaster's data collection.

A counterargument to all this (no pun intended) is that counters can still serve a purpose for those who do not have access to their server logs. Several of the sites that I run do have counters on them (see Figure 2–5) since I use a private ISP and cannot access the logs. The counter that appears on this page is the only way I have to see how many people have visited my site. In these cases, the counters are for my own information.

Figure 2–7: Privacy policy Web page of eBay

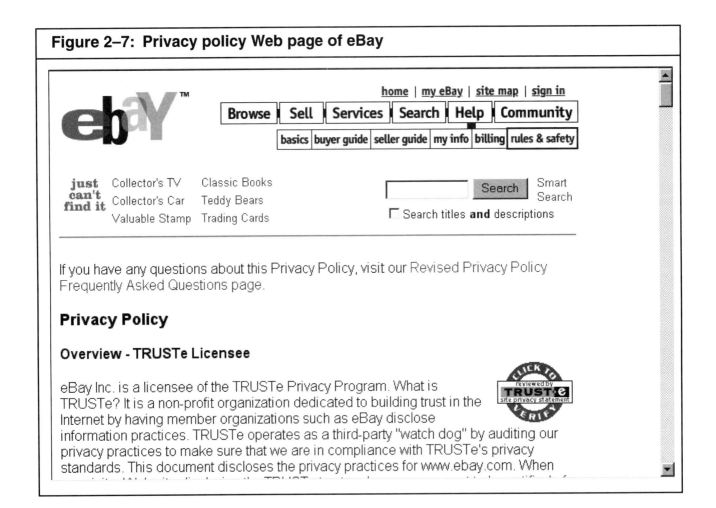

- **Awards**
  Several years ago Internet awards actually meant something. One of my Web sites was even a "Cool Site of the Day" once. This has changed. These days, with such sites as "cool site of the second" and others, awards have been devalued to the point of practical worthlessness. If you wish to take a site's awards into consideration (see Figure 2–6 for example), make sure of one thing—that you have even heard of the organization/site issuing the award.
- **Privacy Policy**
  If a site collects information from its users, many users require that the site have a posted privacy policy (see Figure 2–7) that states what information is collected and what will, and will not, be done with that information. The lack of such a policy may be cause to avoid that site.

At this point you are probably thinking to yourself, "Well, you've left me with nothing, since no Internet resource passes each of these evaluations." Well, that is not entirely true. Individual elements may not be *completely* reliable, but that does not mean that all of them taken as a larger whole cannot be useful. I only mean to stress that no single element should be considered in isolation. A final determination of the worth of a document can only be made after weighing all of the relevant issues.

EVALUATION EXERCISES

Here are some Web sites that may help to answer a few sample reference questions. First I'll give you the question, then point you to a site that you might find when searching for a site to answer that question. (The URLs for the sites follow each question and can also be found hyperlinked on this book's Web site.) Take a look at the site and evaluate it. The ultimate question in each example is "Is this a site that I should recommend to my patron to use to answer his or her question?"

Question: "I'm thinking about moving to Mankato, Minnesota. Can you find some information for me on that town?"

Site: The Mankato Minnesota Home Page
             www.lme.mankato.msus.edu/mankato/mankato.html

Question: "I am doing a research project on eccentricities. Can you find any studies for me?"

Site: "A Fundamentally Eccentric Premise" by L.X. Finegold
             www.improbable.com/archives/paperair/volume6/v6i6/fundamentally-6-6.html

Question: "I'm doing research on the backlash to women's rights. Do you have any information on that?"

Site: Ladies Against Women
             www.well.com/user/gail/ladies/

Figure 2–8: The Mankato, MN, Web site URL

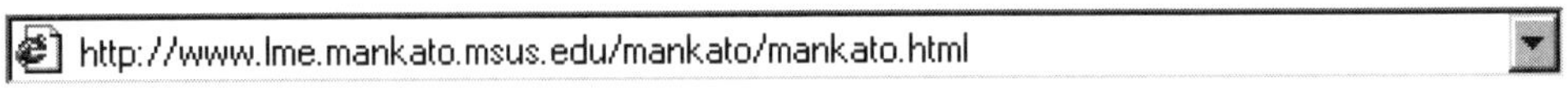

| http://www.lme.mankato.msus.edu/mankato/mankato.html |

Question: "I've heard that the chemical dihydrogen monoxide is bad for you. What can you tell me about it?"
Site: Dihydrogen Monoxide Research Division
             www.dhmo.org/

Question: "I'm a student linguist researching obscure languages from south of the equator. What information do you have about that?"
Site: A Concise Grammar of Feorran
             www.fortunecity.com/rivendell/everquest/624/feorran.html

---

REVIEWING YOUR EVALUATION EXERCISES

Go through all of the exercises on your own first. Take note of what you noticed about each site that makes you question its validity. When you are done, proceed through this next section to see what you may have missed.

MANKATO, MINNESOTA

In the case of the Mankato, MN, homepage there are a couple of key items you should be looking at.

- **The URL**
  The URLs for cities in the United States are usually in the following format: *www.ci.cityname.state.us*. This one, however, is located at an educational institution (see Figure 2–8). Maybe the city doesn't have enough funds to run their own systems and the local college volunteered. Maybe, but is it likely?
- **Mankato's history**
  Not exactly the history most would expect. This history starts out by mentioning an "Underwater City" and "Gods who arrived in the area in great silver glowing disks."

Figure 2–9: The "sponsor" of the Mankato, MN, site

Florida Voters Guide!

Please patronize our sponsors! (They will patronize you.)

Attention Florida, dead, missing, illegal alian voters. A wonderful new book for you! Available at my local book dealer.

Figure 2–10: The mayor of Mankato, MN, site

The Honorable Cristy *"Fast Eddie"* Swindler

Faux-Mayor Swindler

I want to welcome you all to Mankato, Minnesota. Trust me, I am your mayor. We like to call Mankato "The City to Build In". We will allow you to build anything, anywhere and do anything with it you want! Yes, we are a friendly town! And *I run it...*

We have recently acquired a new snow plow. It cost lots of money. We are very careful. We will not use it in the winter. In this way, the streets will remain impassible - except by my house - and we will not

Figure 2–11: Abridgment statement from "A Fundamentally Eccentric Premise"

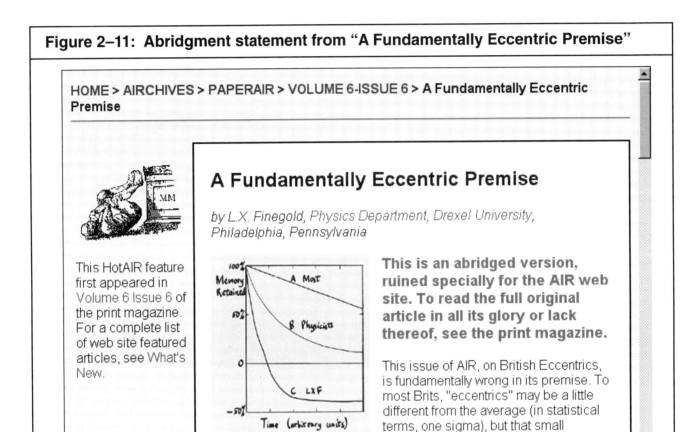

HOME > AIRCHIVES > PAPERAIR > VOLUME 6-ISSUE 6 > A Fundamentally Eccentric Premise

A Fundamentally Eccentric Premise

by L.X. Finegold, Physics Department, Drexel University, Philadelphia, Pennsylvania

This HotAIR feature first appeared in Volume 6 Issue 6 of the print magazine. For a complete list of web site featured articles, see What's New.

This is an abridged version, ruined specially for the AIR web site. To read the full original article in all its glory or lack thereof, see the print magazine.

This issue of AIR, on British Eccentrics, is fundamentally wrong in its premise. To most Brits, "eccentrics" may be a little different from the average (in statistical terms, one sigma), but that small difference is perfectly acceptable and

- **The photos**
  The photos throughout the site are plentiful. The problem is that no two of them seem to be from the same place, though all claim to be taken in Mankato.
- **The site's sponsor**
  If you take a look at the sponsorship of this page (see Figure 2–9), it is not exactly a real sponsor.
- **The language**
  The language of the site is quite non-professional to say the least. Numerous spelling errors are also noticeable.
- **The mayor**
  His nickname is "Fast Eddie" and his photo is a mug shot (see Figure 2–10). Be sure to notice the name of his secretary.
- **The other Mankato homepage**
  Clicking on this link will get you to the real site for the city located at *www.ci.mankato.mn.us/*. Instantly you get the feeling that you have reached the correct location.

Figure 2–12: References from "A Fundamentally Eccentric Premise"

References

Cook, J., 1779. English are called Limeys because Captain James Cook (he used to live near me) pioneered lime fruit for his sailors, to ward off scurvy. With typical British efficiency, he chose the citrus fruit lowest in the anti-scurvy Vitamin C. So the English are no longer scurvy knaves... But I digress.

Finegold, L.X., 2000. Personal interview with LXF, 1 IV 2000.

Macdonald, J.A., 1867. He used to live near where I got hitched.

Onymous, A.N., 2000. I memorized this one. Sorry, can't find author. It's an oldie.

Weeks, Dr. D. and J. James, 1996. *Eccentrics: A study of Sanity and Strangeness*, Kodansha International, New York, p. 105.

© *Copyright 2000 Annals of Improbable Research (AIR)*

HOME > AIRCHIVES > PAPERAIR > VOLUME 6-ISSUE 6 > A Fundamentally Eccentric Premise

---

Conclusion: This site is not of any use to anyone that wishes to learn about Mankato, Minnesota, and therefore not a reliable reference resource.

"A FUNDAMENTALLY ECCENTRIC PREMISE" BY L.X. FINEGOLD

Upon the first reading of this article you may wonder if the author is serious or not and even if this was "real" research. Here's what you can find:

- **The document title**
  Taking a quick look at the title of the document (see Figure 2–11), and the first part, HotAIR, you get the impression that this may be bogus.
- **Abridgment**
  The document does state that it is an abridgment of the version in the print magazine. The fact that there is a print

Figure 2–13: Homepage from The Annals of Improbable Research

version may lend credence to the information. Then again, maybe it doesn't.

- **References**
  This research paper does include references (see Figure 2–12) and that is a good sign upon first glance. Upon reading the references themselves however, this is no longer the case. Only the last citation is at all serious or relevant. The second in fact is the author interviewing himself.

- **The Annals of Improbable Research**
  Clicking on the home link at the top of the page will take you to the homepage of the journal that is presenting this research: The Annals of Improbable Research (see Figure 2–13). This is not necessarily a reassuring title for someone looking for serious research.

- **About AIR**
  From the homepage you can click on the "About AIR" link (see Figure 2–14) to find out a little more about the

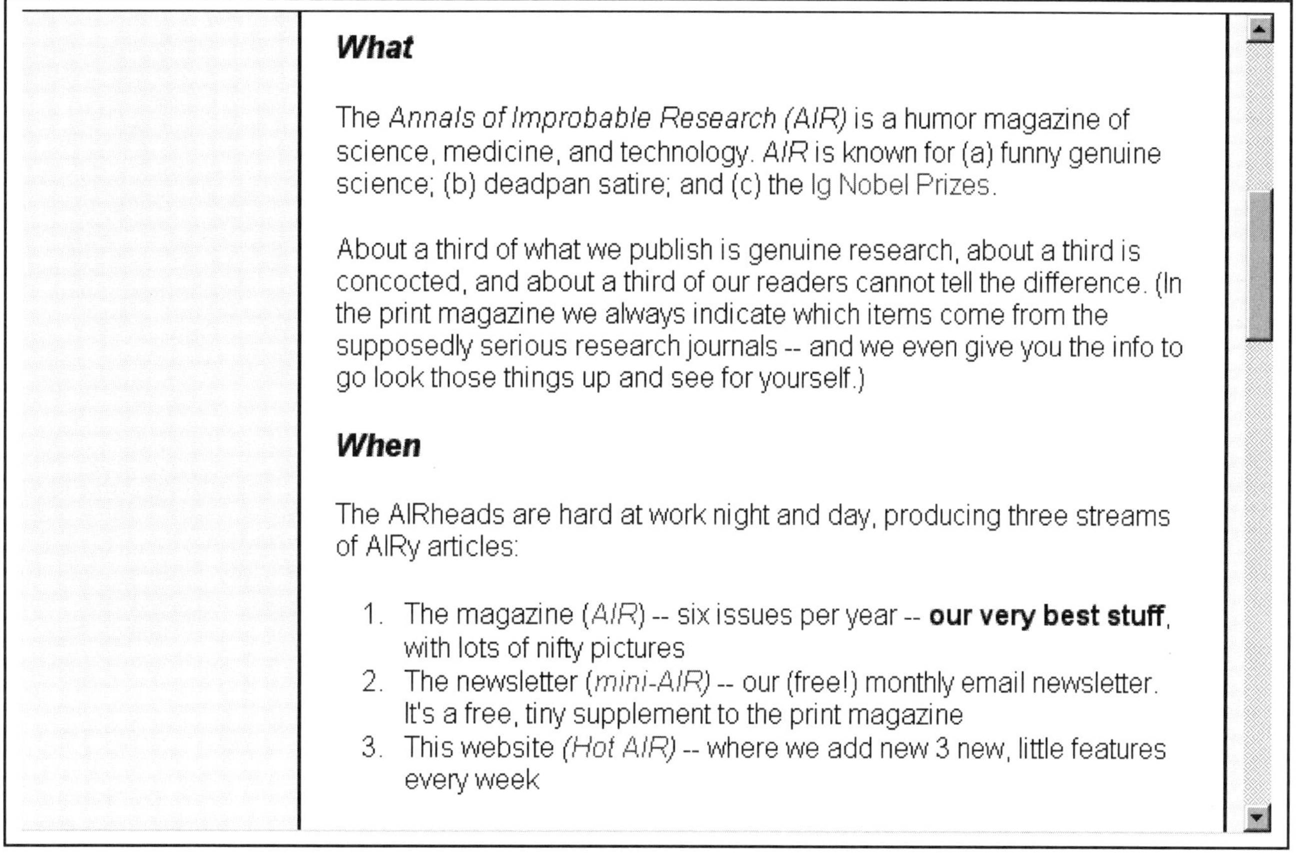

Figure 2–14: "About" page on the AIR Web site

What

The *Annals of Improbable Research (AIR)* is a humor magazine of science, medicine, and technology. *AIR* is known for (a) funny genuine science; (b) deadpan satire; and (c) the Ig Nobel Prizes.

About a third of what we publish is genuine research, about a third is concocted, and about a third of our readers cannot tell the difference. (In the print magazine we always indicate which items come from the supposedly serious research journals -- and we even give you the info to go look those things up and see for yourself.)

When

The AIRheads are hard at work night and day, producing three streams of AIRy articles:

1. The magazine (*AIR*) -- six issues per year -- **our very best stuff**, with lots of nifty pictures
2. The newsletter (*mini-AIR*) -- our (free!) monthly email newsletter. It's a free, tiny supplement to the print magazine
3. This website *(Hot AIR)* -- where we add new 3 new, little features every week

---

journal itself. The "about" page does state that the journal is a "humor magazine . . . known for funny genuine science [and] deadpan satire . . ." It goes on to state, "about a third of what we publish is genuine research, about a third is concocted, and about a third of our readers cannot tell the difference." This leads us to conclude that the article just may be legitimate. According to this page, the printed journal indicates which items are serious and which are not.

- **Issue table of contents**
  Lastly we can check the table of contents (see Figure 2–15) for the issue in which the article appears. You can find the table by clicking on the "volume 6-issue 6" link on the article page. This page states "features marked with a star (*) are based entirely on material taken from standard research (and other Official and Therefore Always

Figure 2–15: Table of contents for the November-December 2000 issue of the AIR Web site

The features marked with a star (*) are based entirely on material taken straight from standard research (and other Official and Therefore Always Correct) literature. Many of the other articles are genuine, too, but we don't know which ones.

Special Section: ECCENTRICS

- 4 Edward D. Cope, Heads Above the Rest, the First Electronic Publisher in Science* *Earle E. Spamer*
- 6 The Gentle Art of Political Taxidermy: Charles Waterton, Squire of Walton Hall* *Sally Shelton*
- 10 Chonosuke Okamura, Visionary* *Earle E. Spamer*
- 12 A Fundamentally Eccentric Premise* *L.X. Finegold*
- 14 Eccentric Research Recommendations* *Stephen Drew*
- 15 Frank "Bring 'Em Back Alive and Ready to Eat" Buckland* *Sally Shelton*
- 17 Decoding the British ack-SEN-triks Movement: A Phonemological Analysis* *Harold P. Dowd*

Medical Breakthroughs

- 20 AIRhead Medical Review* -- *Bertha Vanatian*
- 21 *The HMO-NO News:* Spiff Up Your Image!

AIRhead Research Roundup*

- 19 AIRhead Research Review* *Dirk Manley*

Correct) literature." Finding the article in question on this page you will see that it is marked with an asterisk.

Conclusion: This is a legitimate, although humorous document. It may not be best to use this as the sole source for the research paper in question but it may have its place. At a minimum, since this is an abridgment of the article, the full article should be found for the patron.

LADIES AGAINST WOMEN

For Ladies Against Women (see Figure 2–16), whether or not you agree with the author's statements, the key is to figure out if the author is serious. Here's what you should look at:

- **Who is the author of this document**
  Her name is Gail. (Look at the URL.) But does that help?

Figure 2–16: Homepage of the Ladies Against Women Web site

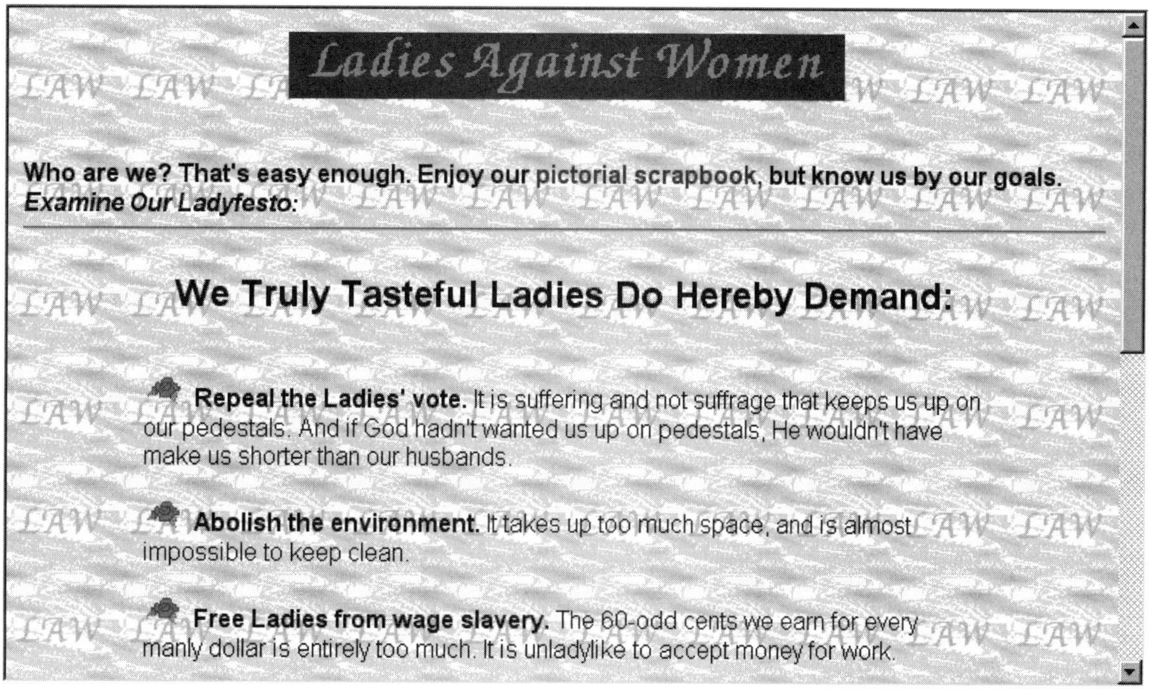

- Links
  None of the links on this document will help you determine its legitimacy. Though that does not ultimately determine anything (it could just be a poorly designed site) it is something to consider. You would hope that at least one of the links on the page would assist you in establishing the context of this page. Unfortunately, they do not.
- Context
  What you're left with is a dead end. When that happens try deconstructing the URL. Delete everything after "gail/" and then press your enter key. You will end up on a page (see Figure 2–17) that tells you all about Gail and what she does: political comedy.

Conclusion: The page in question is satire and not meant to be taken seriously and therefore not a reliable reference resource.

Figure 2–17: About the Author of the Ladies Against Women Web Site

We each bring a series of metaphors to any group endeavor, and in a place made of words, they are one of our most important offerings. All of my experience is food for thought and actions online, from my early days in Canyon, and as a young explorer in the Palisades, on the Eastern Sierra Crest, where my family ran a mountaineering school.

And my political comedy days, spent mostly as Virginia Cholesterol of Ladies Against Women (here snapped outside the 1984 Republican National Convention by Book of the Subgenius author Doug Smith. We were doing a Bake Sale for the Deficit featuring "twinkies from scratch" at the time.) Besides performing, there were years of producing touring stage shows and curious events like this one, coordinating media adventures, composing satirical press releases, performing and directing others, and doing community-building for my own and other troupes.

Doing improv on the sidewalk is an awful lot like posting online. Of course, we called flaming "heckling" if they did it real-time, and "criticism" if they printed it!

Figure 2–18: The title and URL for the DHMO Web page

DIHYDROGEN MONOXIDE RESEARCH DIVISION

A quick search on the name of the chemical dihydrogen monoxide in most major search engines will find this site and others, including many that seek to ban the chemical. This site seems to present a more balanced treatment of the issues.

- **The URL**
  Taking a look at the URL (see Figure 2–18) shows you this site is run by a nonprofit organization.
- **Site content**
  The site (see Figure 2–19) claims to be an "unbiased data clearinghouse" of information on this chemical unlike other sites that can be found that openly promote the banning of this substance. Upon further investigation, many of the documents make claims that present DHMO in a negative light, including the t-shirts available in their online store.
- **The disclaimer**
  At the bottom of the homepage (see Figure 2–20) is the following statement: "Note: content veracity not implied." This may lead you to believe that something is a little fishy.
- **Dihydrogen monoxide**
  The site never gives a formula for this chemical, which is a little odd. The formula is in fact H_2O, which would lead you to its more common name. This site and others are presenting significantly skewed information about water.

Conclusion: Although all or most of the statements and claims in the site are true, the site should not be used as the basis of serious research. It can, however, be used to allay the patron's fears about dihydrogen monoxide.

A CONCISE GRAMMAR OF FEORRAN

Finally, you're presented with a linguistic study of an Antarctic language. Assuming you know nothing about linguistics, what can you look at to help you out?

- **The subject of the document**
  When was the last time you heard of people ever living on Antarctica? I am sure you have never heard it because there was never an indigenous population on that continent (unless the penguins have learned to talk).

Figure 2–19: The "unbiased" statement of the DHMO.org homepage

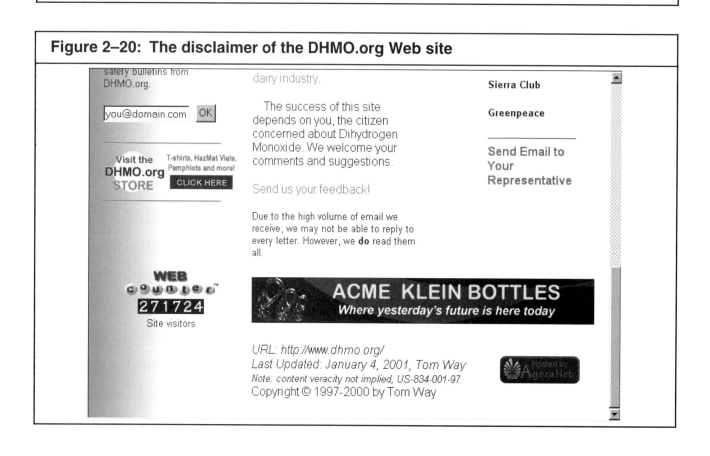

Figure 2–20: The disclaimer of the DHMO.org Web site

Figure 2–21: The homepage of Fortune City

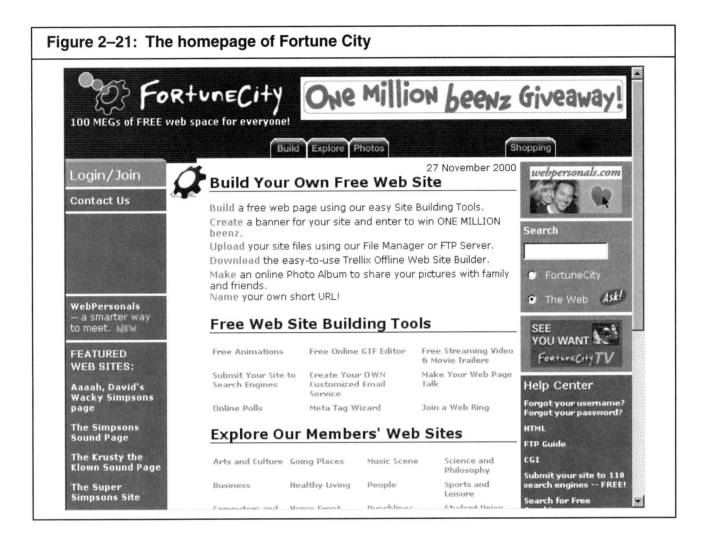

- **The FortuneCity URL**
  Would someone who has done such an important study post it on a "free web site" hosting service? You would probably expect this document (see Figure 2–21) to be hosted at an institution of higher learning (.edu in the United States). Again, this does not automatically invalidate the document but it might be an important clue. To find out, deconstruct the URL. This time, you are best off removing everything back to the main domain.
- **Rivendell**
  One other part of the URL that a few people notice is the word "Rivendell." If this caused you to think of the works of J.R.R. Tolkien (Rivendell is the home of the elves), you are on the right track. For his Hobbit and Lord of the

---

Figure 2–22: The acknowledgements for the Feorran study

Acknowledgements

This work was funded in part by the American Science Foundation (ASF Grant:#94-184061); by a grant from the Graduate Student Research Fund of Northern Indiana University; and by a grant from the Antarctic Studies Trust Fund. I am grateful to each of these for their support.

I wish to thank my advisors, Frederic W. Gleach, Greg Anderson, and Mary Swinson. Without their advice, this work could not have been done. I also wish to thank the United States Navy for their generous support at McMurdo Station. I want to express my gratitude to the government of New Zealand for giving me permission to work with the Tôlte. I cannot fail to thank my many friends in the Tôlte nation, especially the Shaman Soqhai. All errors are my own.

Table of Contents

1. Introduction
2. Phonology
3. Morphology:Introduction
4. Nominal Morphology
5. Pronominal Morphology
6. Verbal Morphology
7. Morphology: Miscellaneous
8. Uninflected Word Classes
9. Syntax (Incomplete)
10. Texts (Not yet posted.)

Rings books, Tolkien created whole languages for his characters to use.

- **The Acknowledgements (see Figure 2–22)**
There are a few odd items here, most notably the reference to "The American Science Foundation." That organization is actually known as the "National Science Foundation" or NSF.
- **Who is being cited in this work?**
One of the individuals mentioned in the citations is "William Q. Burrows." Some of the students in my class have noticed that this sounds a lot like "William S. Burroughs" the author of *Naked Lunch*. In fact, the mentioned indi-

Figure 2–23: Works cited in the Feorran study

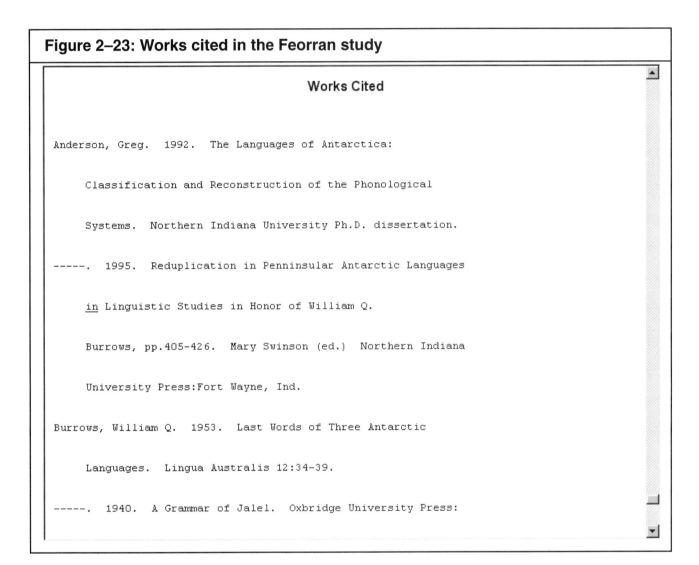

Works Cited

Anderson, Greg. 1992. The Languages of Antarctica:

    Classification and Reconstruction of the Phonological

    Systems. Northern Indiana University Ph.D. dissertation.

-----. 1995. Reduplication in Penninsular Antarctic Languages

    in Linguistic Studies in Honor of William Q.

    Burrows, pp.405-426. Mary Swinson (ed.) Northern Indiana

    University Press:Fort Wayne, Ind.

Burrows, William Q. 1953. Last Words of Three Antarctic

    Languages. Lingua Australis 12:34-39.

-----. 1940. A Grammar of Jalel. Oxbridge University Press:

viduals is actually a play on the name of the famous author according to the creator of this site.

- **Context/Conlang link at the bottom of the page**
This link will take you to a page by the same author (see Figure 2–24), which explains that this site is completely made up, and why he did it. Without clicking on this link, most readers will only be skeptical at best.

Conclusion: If the patron is doing research on Antarctica this is not a reliable resource. However, if the patron is interested in languages and linguistics in general this may be an informative document.

Figure 2–24: The homepage of Brad's Conlang and Conculture Pages

Brad's

Conlang and Conculture Pages

UPDATE: I have been remiss in working on these pages for sometime. I am now (6/13/2000) writing new pages and preparing to edit and rework some of the ones presently located here.

Welcome to my conlang and conculture pages. What is a conlang? Simply put it is a language that is artificially constructed by someone or some group. A conculture is the imaginary culture invented to go along with that language. Famous examples include Tolkien's Elvish languages and Middle Earth or more recently, the Klingons of Star Trek fame. Not all conlangs are supported by concultures, examples include Esperanto, Interlingua, and Lojban.

I have invented several languages over the years and most of them have had concultures attached to them. Only a few are available on the web at this time. **Nova** is my most developed project. It includes a fairly large dictionary, a grammar, some texts, and a large number of pages devoted to the culture and natural history of the island on which it is found.
Feorran is a newer project. Feorran has a smallish dictionary, a grammatical sketch, and an ethnographic sketch of the conculture. Feorran was originally intended to be a closed end project but I have enjoyed it so much that I plan to keep working on it.
Other projects that will be added here include **Marata** which exists as only a bare bones sketch of the derivational system, **Nonoaltec**, the working name for a language that will be derived from the real Uto-Aztecan Language Family, and an as yet unnamed family of languages that will be derived from the lost

TEACHING EVALUATION SKILLS TO PATRONS

Knowing how to successfully evaluate an Internet resource is wonderful from the librarian's standpoint. In one way or another this information needs to be passed on to your patrons. Since many patrons feel that the Internet may be a replacement for asking their questions at the reference desk, we must take it upon ourselves to train them how to differentiate a good resource from a bad one.

In the next section you will find many online resources on the topic of evaluation, many of which are designed specifically for that library's patrons. Take a look at them and use them as a model for your own patron training.

EVALUATION RESOURCES

SITES FOR USE IN EVALUATION EXERCISES

For those interested in using the evaluation exercises for patron or student training, here is a list of recommended sites and others used by Internet trainers all over the world.

Ladies Against Women (*www.well.com/user/gail/ladies/*)
Feline Reactions to Bearded Men (*www.improbable.com/airchives/classical/cat/cat.html*)
DreamTech International (*www.d-b.net/dti/*)
Brain Transplantation (*http://216.247.9.207/ny-best.htm*)
A Concise Grammar of Feorran (*www.fortunecity.com/rivendell/everquest/624/feorran.html*)
Ban Dihydrogen Monoxide (*www.lhup.edu/~dsimanek/dhmo.hth*)
TASS.NET (www.tass.net/)
The Mankato, MN, Home Page (*www.lme.mankato.msus.edu/mankato/mankato.html*)
Whales in the Minnesota River
(*www.nytimes.com/library/tech/99/03/circuits/articles/04trut.html*)
AFDB (*http://zapatopi.net/afdb.html*)
True but Little Known Facts about Women and AIDS (*http://147.129.1/library/research/AIDSFACTS.htm*)
Americans with No Abilities Act (*www.theonion.com/onion3324/noabilities.html*)
William Shakespeare (*www.iue.indiana.edu/library/newlib/wwweval.html*)

Welcome to the White House (*www.whitehouse.net*)
NordiCaLite (*www.ari.net/nordicalite/*)

FOR FURTHER READING

There are many sites on the Web that deal with both the more technical aspects of evaluating Internet resources and more simple guides designed for library patrons. If you are interested in pursuing this topic further or in developing a resource for your patrons, here are many places you can start.

Anyone Can (and Probably Will) Put Anything Up on the Internet (*http://thorplus.lib.purdue.edu/~techman/eval.html*)

Better Read That Again: Web Hoaxes and Misinformation (*www.infotoday.com/searcher/sep00/piper.htm*)

Bibliography on Evaluating Internet Resources (*www.lib.vt.edu/research/libinst/evalbiblio.html*)

Bryn Mawr-Haverford Research Guide 1: Library Research (*www.brynmawr.edu/library/Docs/resguide1.html*)

Critical Thinking and Internet Resources (*www.mcrel.org/resources/plus/critical.asp*)

Critical Thinking in an Online World (*www.library.ucsb.edu/untangle/jones.html*)

Evaluating & Citing Information Found on the Net (*www.jsr.cc.va.us/lrc/evaele.htm*)

Evaluating Information Found on the Internet (*http://milton.mse.jhu.edu:8001/research/education/net.html*)

Evaluating Internet Information (*http://medstat.med.utah.edu/navigator/discovery/eval.html*)

Evaluating Internet Research Sources (*www.vanguard.edu/rharris/evalu8it.htm*)

Evaluating Internet Resources (*www.trinityvt.edu/bdavis/desk/eval.htm*)

Evaluating Internet Resources (*www.lme.mankato.msus.edu/ded/tt/19eval.html*)

Evaluating Internet Resources (*www.library.temple.edu/libinst/neteval.htm*)

Evaluating Internet Sites (*www.lib.purdue.edu/search.html*)

Evaluating Quality on the Net (*www.tiac.net/users/hope/findqual.html*)

Evaluating the Documents You Have Found on the World Wide Web (*www.curtin.edu.au:80/curtin/library/staffpages/gwpersonal/senginestudy/zeval.htm*)

Evaluating the Quality of Internet Information Sources (*http://itech1.coe.uga.edu/Faculty/GWilkinson/webeval.html*)

Evaluating Web Resources (*www2.widener.edu/Wolfgram-Memorial-Library/webeval.htm*)

Evaluating WWW Resources (*www.moorhead.msus.edu/library/instruct/evaluate.htm*)

Evaluation of Information Sources (*www.vuw.ac.nz/~agsmith/evaln/evaln.htm*)

Evaluation of Internet Sites & Internet Research (*www.d-e.pvt.k12.nj.us/Internal/libinter.htm*)

The Good, the Bad, and the Ugly: or Why It's a Good Idea to Evaluate Web Sources (*http://lib.nmsu.edu/staff/susabeck/eval.html*)

How to Critically Analyze Information Sources (*www.library.cornell.edu/ okuref/research/skill26.htm*)

How to Evaluate Internet Resources (*http://falcon.jmu.edu/~maxfiesl/chem/ eval.htm*)

Information Quality: The Internet Guide to Construction of Quality Online Resources (*www.ciolek.com/WWWVL-InfoQuality.html*)

Internet Detective: Interactive Tutorial (*www.sosig.ac.uk/desire/internet-detective.html*)

Internet Source Validation Project (*www.stemnet.nf.ca/Curriculum/Validate/*)

Kathy Schrock's Guide for Educators: Critical Evaluation Surveys (*www.capecod.net/schrockguide/eval.htm*)

Library Selection Criteria for WWW Resources (*http://www6.pilot.infi.net/ ~carolyn/criteria.html*)

NetAware (*http://chiron.valdosta.edu/dlgraf/*)

Practical Steps in Evaluating Internet Resources (*http://milton.mse.jhu.edu: 8001/research/education/practical.html*)

Quality of Information . . . and Disinformation Online (*http://blake.oit.unc.edu/ ~rbstepno/disinfo.html*)

Resource Selection and Information Evaluation (*http://alexia.lis.uiuc.edu/ ~janicke/Evaluate.html*)

Scholarly Publishing and the Fluid World Wide Web (*www.csu.edu.au/special/ conference/apwww95/papers95/atreloar/atreloar.html*)

T is for Thinking (*www.ithaca.edu/library/Training/hott.html*)

Teaching Critical Evaluation Skills for World Wide Web Resources (*www.science.widener.edu/~withers/webeval.htm*)

Teaching Students to Think Critically about Internet Resources (*http:// weber.u.washington.edu/~libr560/NETEVAL/index.html*)

Ten C's for Evaluating Internet Resources (*www.uwec.edu/Admin/Library/ 10cs.html*)

Testing the Surf: Criteria for Evaluating Internet Information Resources (*http:/ /info.lib.uh.edu/pr/v8/n3/smit8n3.html*)

Thinking Critically about World Wide Web Resources (*www.library.ucla.edu/ libraries/college/instruct/web/critical.htm*)

Why We Need to Evaluate What We Find on the Internet (*http://thorplus.lib. purdue.edu/~techman/eval.html*)

3 CREATING AN EFFECTIVE READY REFERENCE STRATEGY

Reference questions can be broken down into two types: ready reference and complex reference. Ready reference questions are commonly defined as any question with a factual answer lacking the need for interpretation and which an experienced reference librarian can answer in five minutes or less. Complex reference questions are those that need more research and whose answers may need interpretation by the person with the question.

In this chapter, I will discuss the strategy necessary to use the Internet to answer ready reference questions in an efficient manner. Chapter 5 will deal with complex reference questions.

REVIEWING YOUR CURRENT PRINT STRATEGY

Let us first consider a sample ready reference question: What is the capital of Zimbabwe?

Ignoring the Internet right now, what would you do to answer this question?

I can guess that you just said the following to yourself: "I'd get the *World Almanac* and look up the Zimbabwe entry."

Now, you may not have come up with the *World Almanac*. Maybe you thought of the *CIA World Factbook*, or an encyclopedia. Regardless of what book you actually chose, the solution you came up with can be distilled into the following two steps:

1. Go to the book
2. Find the answer

In this example those two steps would read:

1. Go to the *World Almanac*
2. Find the Zimbabwe page that has the answer

Now, let's try the same question using the Internet.

You may be saying to yourself, "Why would I ever use the Internet to answer this question when I have the almanac right there?" Well, maybe the almanac is being used by another patron. Maybe the Zimbabwe page has been removed by someone who could not afford the photocopier. Maybe the student "must" find it using the Internet. There are plenty of reasons why you would need to use the Internet. Later we will discuss how to decide when to use the Internet and when to use print.

REVIEWING YOUR CURRENT INTERNET STRATEGY

I've found that most librarians will do the following:

1. Go to favorite search engine
2. Type in *Zimbabwe capital*
3. Click the search button
4. Wait for results
5. Retrieve approximately 1,699,453 results
6. Click on the first result
7. Wait for document to load
8. Don't find answer
9. Back up
10. Click on another result
11. Wait for document to load
12. Don't find answer
13. Repeat until frustrated
14. Try new keywords
15. Wait some more
16. Pick some more results
17. Still don't find answer
18. Try another search engine
19. Give up and go get the *World Almanac*

Sound familiar?

> But of course the Internet *can* work. In some cases you will be able to get the answer from the first site, but how often does that happen to you? Even if it does happen, is it faster than print?
>
> So, the question becomes: what can we do to the Internet to make it, at a minimum, as useful as print is for ready reference questions? If we take it one step further, maybe we can make the Internet more useful than print in certain situations.

CREATING AN EFFECTIVE NEW INTERNET STRATEGY

Our specific example shows the general problem for all ready reference searchers. Let's take a look at those two strategies again. Book Strategy:

1. Go to the book
2. Find the answer

Internet Strategy:

1. Go to favorite search engine
2. Type in keywords
3. Click the search button
4. Wait for results
5. Retrieve too many results
6. Click on the first result
7. Wait for document to load
8. Don't find answer
9. Back up
10. Click on another result
11. Wait for document to load
12. Don't find answer
13. Repeat until frustrated
14. Try new keywords
15. Wait some more
16. Pick some more results
17. Still don't find answer
18. Try another search engine
19. Give up and go get a book

Which one works and which one doesn't?

If your answer was that the print strategy works and the Internet one does not, you're absolutely right. (If what you were doing on the Internet worked, you probably wouldn't be reading this book.)

The next question is, what can we do to that Internet strategy to make it work as well as, if not, better than print?

Before I propose an alternative strategy for using the Internet, let me rephrase your current print strategy:

1. Go to resource
2. Find answer

Phrased like this, I have now become technologically neutral. I do not necessarily mean print or Internet. So, let us take that and apply it to the Internet:

1. Go to the site
2. Find answer

I can see that skeptical look on your face already. "What does he mean, 'go to the site, find answer'? Is he nuts?" Well, bear with me for just a few more minutes and let me see if I can convince you. Sometimes the obvious answer is the most difficult to see.

Let's take a final look at those two strategies again.

Book Strategy:

1. Go to the book
2. Find the answer

Internet Strategy:

1. Go to favorite search engine
2. Type in keywords
3. Click the search button
4. Wait for results
5. Retrieve too many results
6. Click on the first result
7. Wait for document to load
8. Don't find answer
9. Back up
10. Click on another result
11. Wait for document to load
12. Don't find answer
13. Repeat until frustrated

Saying that the Internet strategy is faster assumes that you have a fast working connection to the Internet. I once presented this workshop to a group of librarians from the Colorado Department of Corrections. When I asked what their first step was to using the Internet they responded "unlock the cage with the computer in it." Obviously such an unusual step will increase the time needed to use the Internet.

14. Try new keywords
15. Wait some more
16. Pick some more results
17. Still don't find answer
18. Try another search engine
19. Give up and go get a book

Ask yourself this question: At which point did I start treating the Internet differently than print?

The answer to this question is at step one, right at the beginning. You knew instantly what resource you needed in print. Why didn't you know what resource to use on the Internet?

When you examine this strategy and compare it to the one you use for print, which one may actually become faster?

Book Strategy:

1. Go to the book
2. Find the answer

Internet Strategy:

1. Go to site
2. Find answer

The answer is the Internet.

This is where the skepticism always sets in. I know what you are thinking and you are not alone. "Sure. That's easy for him to say. But how do I know what sites to go to? He's the one with all the experience using the Internet. How am I ever going to be able to do that?"

Before you toss this book out of your hand let me tell you how to get there. But first, I'd like to take you back to your first day as a reference librarian.

Do you remember your first day at a reference desk? Was it a little stressful? Did you know what book in your collection had the answer you were looking for? Even if you knew that the almanac had the answer, did you know where the almanac was? One student of mine answered these questions with this answer: "At the end of the day I went home and cried." Many of you can probably relate to that "first day on the job" frustration.

I remember my first time working at a reference desk. I was the graduate assistant to the network services librarian at the University at Albany. I helped make sure the computers on the desks of library faculty and staff worked and that they had all the necessary software installed. One day the head of reference came over to my office (I worked for the reference department) and asked me to cover the reference desk unexpectedly. A little nervously, I stepped behind the desk wanting to do a great job but unsure of my ability to locate the right reference books.

That can be an uncomfortable feeling that might produce an awkward situation. I'm willing to bet that this is how you feel about the Internet today. It is there and you have to do it, but you're lost as to where to go, sometimes even how to start. But remember, you slowly and steadily learned the skills to find print resources. The same challenge will be true for the Internet.

How did you learn print resources? Chances are you did it with practice and experience. This is exactly what you need to do with the Internet.

The last time you used a print resource that you were not very familiar with to answer a reference question, did you take a few moments to check out that resource after the patron walked away? Did you flip through the pages to see how the book was organized, check out the table of contents, and scan the index? Why did you do these things? You did them so that in the future when you received a question that this resource could answer you would be able to go right to it.

Do you take the time, or are you given the time, to shelf read your collection? Does your library set out new materials for your review?

What I am suggesting is shelf reading the Internet. Remember, the Internet is just a collection of resources that are available to you, just like your print collection. I will agree that the collection on the Internet is much larger than your print collection, but it is still, after all, only a collection of resources.

If you think about it, you get the same questions (or at least the same types of questions) all the time. Every public librarian gets the question about how much a used car is worth. A K–12

Some libraries set aside a few minutes each day in which the staff can scan the shelves and familiarize themselves with the collection. The best example I've seen was a library that had a special shelf set aside behind the reference desk on which all new reference books were placed for two weeks. This gave all of the desk staff the ability to familiarize themselves with the new reference material as it came among and before it became lost in all the other materials.

library may get questions about dissecting a frog every spring. Knowing this, what do you do? You prepare.

Here's a great example from the public library world. Every fall, one local teacher gives her students an assignment that is supposed to teach the children how to use their local public library. The child needs to answer 10 to 20 questions. When the first child first shows a librarian these questions, what is the first thing the librarian does? She asks the child to borrow the sheet of questions for a minute and runs over to the photocopier to make a copy. The librarian will then dutifully help the child find all the answers, keeping a copy of the answers on the photocopied question sheet.

The librarian will then keep this sheet of questions and answers at the reference desk, informing all of the other librarians of its existence so that they will not need to spend as much time with other students of the class.

Whether or not this strategy actually helps the rest of the children is not the point of this story. The point is that because the librarian knows that these questions will come up again in the future, the librarian prepares to answer them again.

For these questions, the reference staff is at the two-step process: go to resource (in this case the photocopied sheet) and find the answer.

So, if you take the time to prepare, think about what questions you will be getting in the future, and find the resources to answer those questions ahead of time, you will eventually be able to use the two-step strategy with the Internet.

The next time you're on the Internet not seeming to do anything work related and your boss asks what you are doing, do not respond with "surfing." Tell your boss that you're "shelf reading."

IMPLEMENTING AN EFFECTIVE INTERNET STRATEGY

Now that you have been introduced to my strategy for answering ready reference questions using the Internet, you may be asking yourself how you can implement it. Fine, you now know of sites that can answer different questions but how can you get back to them quickly and painlessly? When asked this question, most will reply quickly, "Bookmarks!"

BOOKMARKS

Bookmarks in Netscape (*favorites* in Internet Explorer) can be a great way to "remember" sites for future quick retrieval. Just by finding a site and then adding a bookmark you can easily return to that site in the future. In theory, bookmarks allow you to pull off the new strategy.

By finding and evaluating the sites that will answer questions that you just know will be asked, you can build an impressive list of bookmarks to help you with the new strategy. Bookmarks can also be organized into subject-oriented hierarchical folders for easy retrieval.

The trouble is that bookmarks in a library setting present several significant problems.

THE PROBLEM WITH BOOKMARKS

Situation one: Ask yourself this: when you click on your bookmarks icon do you see only a long, jumbled list of bookmarks, with a link for "more bookmarks"? Lack of organization can be the single biggest barrier to implementing the new strategy. Taking the time to create folders within your bookmarks and organizing the bookmarks into these folders can overcome this problem. Still, the large number of bookmarks some librarians have can be overwhelming and make it difficult to find the one you need quickly.

> There is another option known as desktop shortcuts in which the browser places an icon on your desktop for quick access to sites. This works best for a limited number of sites that the user accesses very frequently. It is not, therefore, a viable solution for a reference situation.

Situation two: Chances are that you have more than one computer at the reference desk. Do each of these machines have a different set of bookmarks? Now you have to remember which computer has the bookmark you are looking for. What if that computer is in use by another staff member? What if it is down? Any of these problems can slow down your bookmark retrieval time. Creating a single bookmark file on a local network location for access by all reference terminals can solve this problem, but not others.

Situation three: Once you have organized your bookmarks and placed them in a central location for the reference staff, you may still be forgetting one thing: your patrons. Why hide these wonderful resources that you have taken the time to discover and organize behind the reference desk? What about the public access computers? If you use bookmarks only at the reference desk, you are not allowing your patrons access to those bookmarks on the computers they can use. Sure, you can set your browser to access the LAN copy of the bookmarks, but then you have security issues with keeping the patrons from changing those bookmarks. The problems that arise in using bookmarks make them a less-than-ideal solution to the larger problem of general access to your resources.

Situation four: Ultimately, what about your patrons who are not in the library? This is really just an extension of situation three, but in the world of the Internet you must start thinking of patrons as not necessarily physically present. (Colleges and universities started doing this a while ago. Public libraries, with the exception of those with bookmobiles, are just starting to.) Again, you have taken the time to find, evaluate, and organize the resources. Why not make them available to those patrons that are not or cannot be physically in the library? Bookmarks just cannot do this.

So what is the solution?

THE SOLUTION: A WEB-BASED REFERENCE DESK

Creating a Web page, or pages (I'll discuss the differences later), for your reference department is the only solution that will allow you to address all four of the previous situations. A Web page can be easily organized in whatever manner you feel is appropriate (alphabetically, by subject, etc.) and can be accessed by any computer connected to the Internet, whether it be on your refer-

> Unfortunately, there is not enough space in this book to include information on how to write HTML (the language for writing Web pages). However, there are many great free resources online that can get you started with a minimum of effort. I highly recommend Webmonkey at *http://hotwired.lycos.com/webmonkey/ teachingtool/*.

ence desk, a public access computer in the library, or by anyone else with Internet access in the world. (We're not just talking about your local geographic area anymore.)

In telling you that you need to create a Web page, I suggest that you should create *at least* one. Depending on the relevant factors involved, you may need to create multiple pages. For example, some university libraries have a table of contents page that links patrons to subject-based pages (ready reference, science, math, history, biology, computers, etc.), each compiled by someone with subject knowledge and experience. Others have organized their pages based on department or major. Many libraries will also create a local resources page that links patrons to such sites as local news stations and event calendars. Some K–12 libraries create pages specifically designed to point to resources for particular class assignments. How you organize this page or these pages will ultimately depend on your patrons and the types of questions they ask.

All libraries providing reference service need to consider creating their Web pages. There are many wonderful sites to discover and use for cutting-edge ideas. Here are just a few of the best examples of reference pages out there today (see Figures 3–1 to 3–6). URLs are located in Notes and Credits on page 133 and are also hyperlinked at the book's Web site.

> It has been suggested that instead of creating your own pages you can link to those that have been created by others. I believe that this is only a temporary solution since it does not allow you to customize those resources to your library. Another suggestion I received was to create your own pages but to place them on the hard drive of the reference machine. I feel this is also a temporary solution since it does not solve the problems caused by multiple computers and patron access.

Figure 3–1: The Coe College Quick Reference page

Coe College
Stewart Memorial
Library

Library by Paul Engle '31

Library
Home
Coe
Home

Quick Reference Page

QuickLinks: Cedar Rapids, Iowa and Beyond, Dictionaries, Directories,Entertainment, Geography and Travel, GovInfo, Jobs, Medicine,Shopping,Sports,Statistics,Weather, Date and Time

Hours
Loan
Periods
Staff and
Services   **Reference Meta Sites**
Henry
Archives   Galaxy's EINET Reference | IPL Ready Reference Collection | My Virtual Reference Desk |
Chemistry Univ. of Texas at Austin Quick Reference.
Collection
Fisher   **Cedar Rapids, Iowa and Beyond**
Library
Art   Brucemore | Cedar Rapids Web Sites | Cedar Rapids Public Library | Mount Mercy College
Collection Library | Cedar Rapids Symphony | Cedar Rapids Community School District | Cedar Rapids

---

Figure 3–2: The University of Texas at Austin Quick Reference page

Quick Reference

A feature of UT Library Online

THE GENERAL LIBRARIES • THE UNIVERSITY OF TEXAS AT AUSTIN

Major Reference Works
A|B|C|D|E|F|G|H|I|J|K|L|M|N|O|P|Q|R|S|T|U|V|W|X|Y|Z

Reference Resources:
Austin Information
Business Reference
Dictionaries
News and Newspapers
Statistics and Demographics
Telephone and E-Mail Directories
Other Reference Servers

Finding Other Information:
Electronic Books
Electronic Journals
Indexes and Abstracts
Search the Web
Search Usenet Archives
Search UT Austin or UT Phone Directory
UTNetCAT Library Catalog

Major Reference Works

Figure 3–3: The University of Washington Reference Tools by Title page

University Libraries
UNIVERSITY OF WASHINGTON

Information Gateway

Reference Tools by Title

A-C -- D-G -- H-O -- P-T -- U-Z

A - C

Academic 360.com
Academic Press Dictionary of Science & Technology
Altavista Translations
Amazon.com Books
American Art Directory
American FactFinder
American Heritage Book of English Usage
American Heritage Dictionary
American School Directory
American University Home Pages
America's Job Bank

Figure 3–4: The University at Buffalo Reference Sources on the Net page

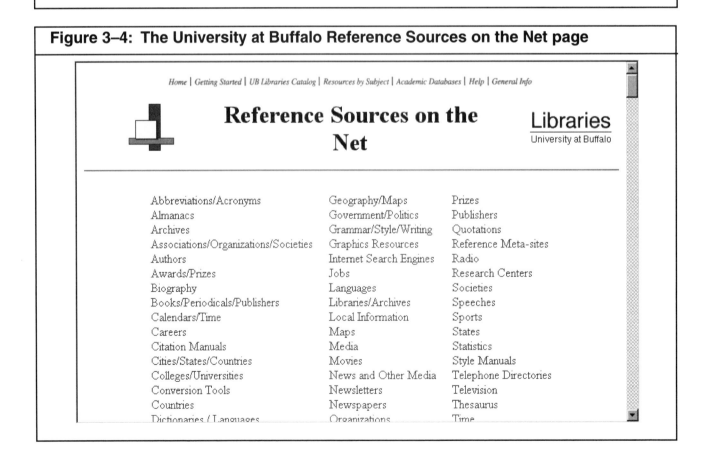

Home | Getting Started | UB Libraries Catalog | Resources by Subject | Academic Databases | Help | General Info

Reference Sources on the Net

Libraries
University at Buffalo

Abbreviations/Acronyms	Geography/Maps	Prizes
Almanacs	Government/Politics	Publishers
Archives	Grammar/Style/Writing	Quotations
Associations/Organizations/Societies	Graphics Resources	Reference Meta-sites
Authors	Internet Search Engines	Radio
Awards/Prizes	Jobs	Research Centers
Biography	Languages	Societies
Books/Periodicals/Publishers	Libraries/Archives	Speeches
Calendars/Time	Local Information	Sports
Careers	Maps	States
Citation Manuals	Media	Statistics
Cities/States/Countries	Movies	Style Manuals
Colleges/Universities	News and Other Media	Telephone Directories
Conversion Tools	Newsletters	Television
Countries	Newspapers	Thesaurus
Dictionaries / Languages	Organizations	Time

Figure 3–5: The University of California at Berkeley Electronic Reference Resources page

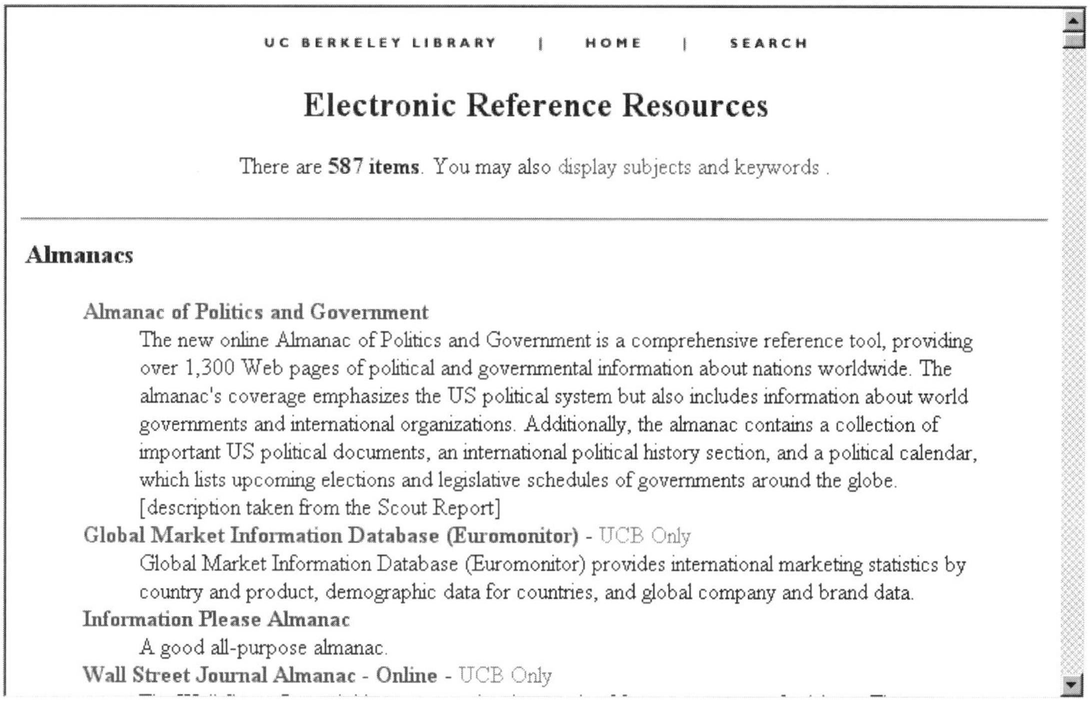

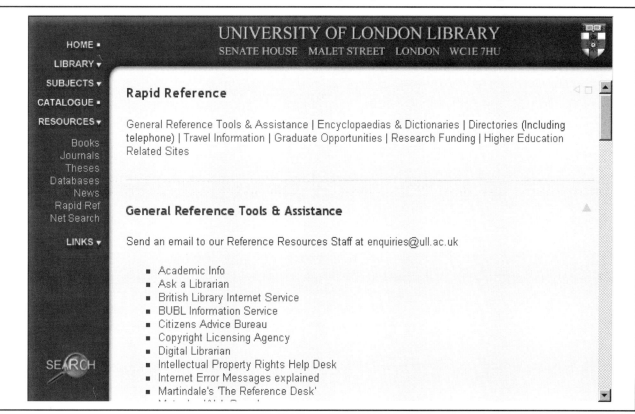

Figure 3–6: The University of London Library Rapid Reference page

REFERENCE WEB PAGE PLACEMENT

Once you have created your pages, you must then decide where the pages should be placed on your library's Web server. I do not mean physical placement within the directory structure of the server's hard drive, I mean where in the site the reference page(s) will be placed so that your patrons (and you) can find it. Many times I have seen great pages that show hours and hours of work on the part of the library staff but are almost impossible to find in the site. Consider the following when deciding where to place your page(s):

1. Make this page the homepage for the computers at the reference desk. When you do this, your resources page will load first when you start the browser and can be quickly accessed with one click of the browser's home button.
2. The resources page should be one click away from the library's main page, and the library's main page should be the homepage for the public access computers in the library. This way, patrons in the library are within one (maybe two) clicks of the reference page at all times.
3. The library's main page should be only one click away from the institution's main page. If you are a university library, your site should be listed on the university's main page. If you're a city's public library, the library should be one click away from the city's main page. I'll admit, I'm a little biased on this issue but I believe that the library is the institution's central information resource and should be able to be found and accessed quickly and easily. Too many times I have seen university libraries hiding under "departments" or, worse, "computing and information resources." When I get to the university's Web site, I want to see a link named "library." Once the "library" link is listed on the institution's main page, patrons from outside the library will be able to find the resources within about three clicks.

> Getting the library site listed on the institution's main page is easier said than done. Local politics may inhibit your ability to easily pull this off. I would argue that it is a battle worth fighting. The easier it is for your patrons to find you, the more they will use you.

READY REFERENCE EXERCISES

Now that you have been introduced to the new strategy and know the steps necessary to implement that strategy, how about giving it a try? How would you try to answer the following sample of ready reference questions using the Internet? Look ahead to the full list of recommended sites on page 73 or refer to the hyperlinked list on the book's Web site and treat the list as if it were your library's reference resources page. Which of those sites might you search to answer the following ready reference questions?

READY REFERENCE QUESTIONS

1. Do any words rhyme with orange?
2. How many other words don't have any rhymes?
3. What does this symbol mean?

4. What does the German word "helfen" mean in English?
5. Where did Samuel Clemens get his pseudonym?
6. What is the equation for the chi^2 test?
7. I'm thinking of purchasing a plot of land. The old man who is selling it says that the size of the plot is 3 hectares. How many acres is that?
8. What time is it?

READY REFERENCE ANSWERS

For each of the questions above this section will do the following:

- give you the answer to the question;
- tell you which site you should have used to find this answer;
- offer the best (most efficient) way to have used that site to find the answer;
- list the problems that I have found to be typical with answering the question;
- tell why the Internet is a better solution for finding the answer to this question than a print equivalent.

Figure 3–7: Rhyme Zone search result

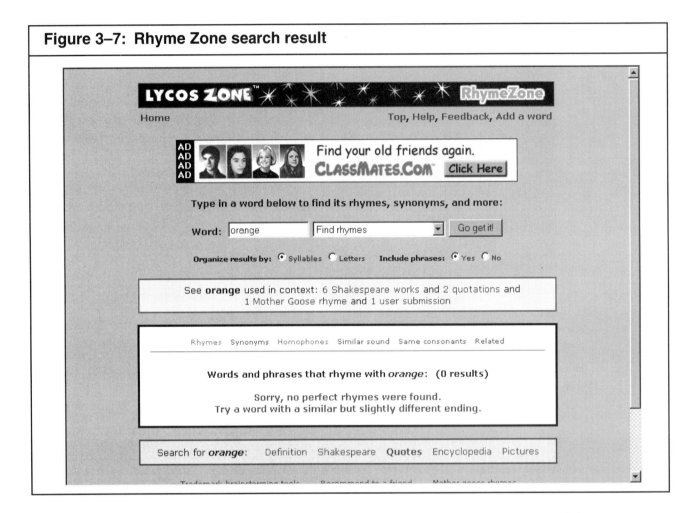

One important note: with the inherent nature of the Internet to change, the following information is current as of the writing of this book, especially the "best method" section. By the time you are doing these exercises this information may no longer be accurate.

Let's find the answers using the Internet. Log on and visit the following sites with this book in hand.

1. *Do any words rhyme with orange?*

Answer:
  No.

Site Used:
  Rhyme Zone, available at: *www.rhymezone.com/*

Best Method (see Figure 3–7):
　Search the site for "orange."

Typical Pitfalls:
　Many feel that when they receive a result that no matches were found, something went wrong with their search. In this case, the zero result is completely accurate.

Why the Internet:
　Unless the library's rhyming dictionary is sitting at the desk, getting to and searching the site will be much quicker.

2.　*How many other words don't have rhymes?*

Answer:
　Three: silver, purple, and month.

Site Used:
　Absolute Trivia, available at *www.absolutetrivia.com/*

Best Method (see Figure 3–8):
　In answering question one we learned that the word *orange* is certainly unusual in the fact that no other word rhymes with it. If we were to find a document mentioning words without rhymes it should mention the word *orange*. Search for *rhyme and orange*.

Typical Pitfalls:
　In this case, just picking the site is the problem. The user's first reaction would probably be to pick the Rhyme Zone as with question one. Unfortunately, there is no way to search that site for this type of answer unless you already know the other three words and just need to confirm the answer. Absolute Trivia is the only other site on the list that could have the answer.

Why the Internet:
　Depending on the size of your collection, you may not have books of trivia in your reference. If you do, they may or may not cover the answer to this question.

Figure 3–8: Absolute Trivia search result

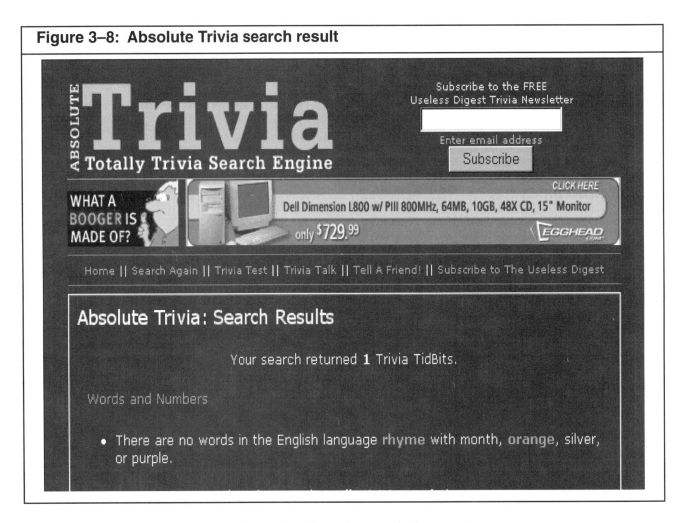

3. *What does this symbol mean?*

Answer:
    The Hand of Fatima

Site Used:
    Symbols of the World, available at *www.symbols.com/*

Best Method (see Figure 3–9):
    Select the graphic index. All that needs to be changed is the open/closed option to "closed," then search. One of the results listed will match the image in question.

Figure 3–9: Symbols of the World search result

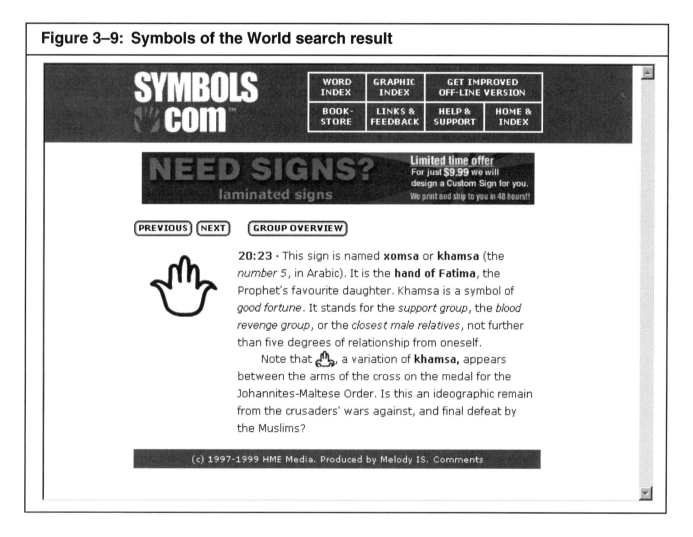

Typical Pitfalls:
In most cases, when presented with the four graphic options, users feel like they have hit a brick wall and go no further or, at best, guess. There are help links that briefly explain what each of the options mean and when to select them. Every user that has tried this question in my workshop and accessed those help screens has said that the help screens were helpful in selecting the correct options for the image.

Why the Internet:
Print symbol dictionaries are not as searchable as this one is. Once the user learns the four options, this site would be much faster than print for this type of question.

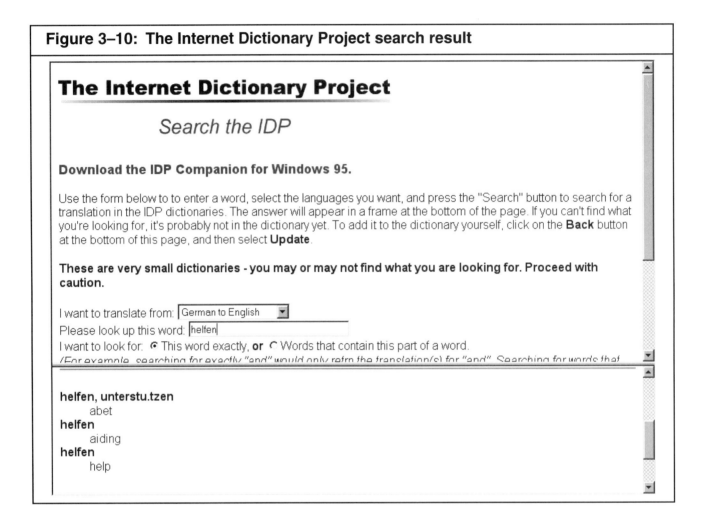

Figure 3–10: The Internet Dictionary Project search result

The Internet Dictionary Project

Search the IDP

Download the IDP Companion for Windows 95.

Use the form below to to enter a word, select the languages you want, and press the "Search" button to search for a translation in the IDP dictionaries. The answer will appear in a frame at the bottom of the page. If you can't find what you're looking for, it's probably not in the dictionary yet. To add it to the dictionary yourself, click on the **Back** button at the bottom of this page, and then select **Update**.

These are very small dictionaries - you may or may not find what you are looking for. Proceed with caution.

I want to translate from: German to English

Please look up this word: helfen

I want to look for: ⦿ This word exactly, **or** ○ Words that contain this part of a word.
(For example, searching for exactly "and" would only retrn the translation(s) for "and". Searching for words that

helfen, unterstu.tzen
    abet
helfen
    aiding
helfen
    help

4. *What does the German word "helfen" mean in English?*

Answer:
  (v.) help, aid, abet

Site Used:
  The Internet Dictionary Project, available at *www.june29.com/ IDP/IDPsearch.html*

Best Method (see Figure 3–10):
  Enter "helfen" into the search box and select "German to English" translation.

Typical Pitfalls:
  The site uses frames and this can confuse some users. If you have a lower-resolution monitor, the answer itself may be off the

Figure 3–11: A&E Biography search result

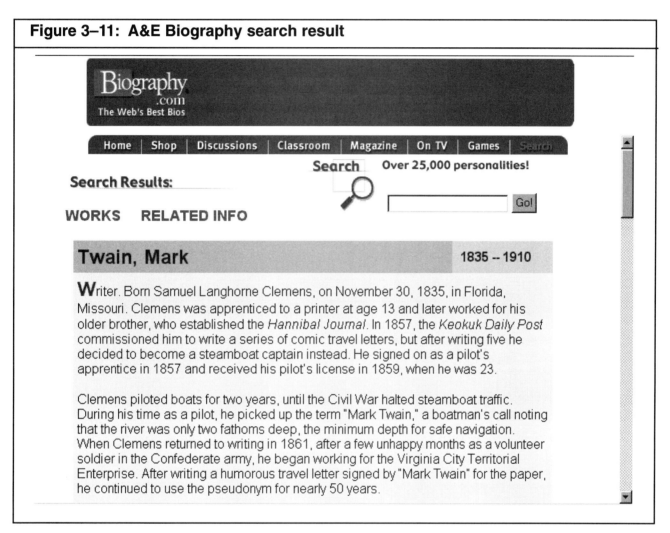

screen; scrolling in the bottom frame would be necessary. This can lead some users to believe that the search was unsuccessful.

Why the Internet:
   Unless the appropriate translation dictionary is within reach, this search is much faster.

5. *Where did Samuel Clemens get his pseudonym?*

Answer:
   "During his time as a [riverboat] pilot, he picked up the term 'Mark Twain,' a boatman's call noting that the river was only two fathoms deep, the minimum depth for safe navigation."

Site Used:
   A&E's Biography.com, available at *www.biography.com/*

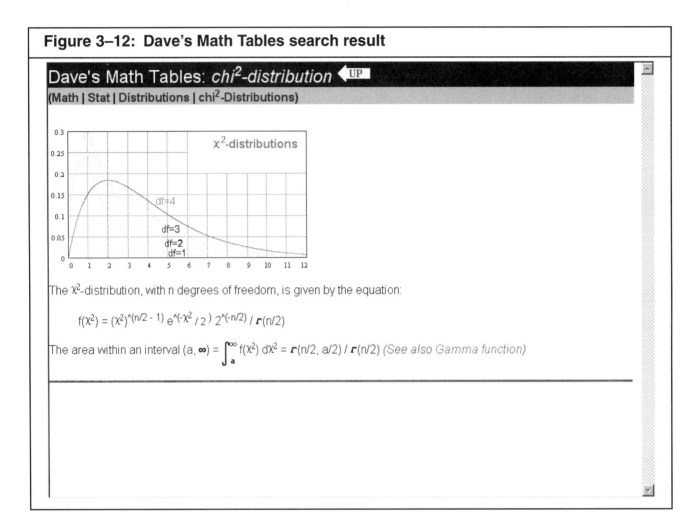

Figure 3–12: Dave's Math Tables search result

Best Method (see Figure 3–11):

Search on "Clemens." Select the result pointing you to "Mark Twain."

Typical Pitfalls:

When searching on "Clemens," users are provided with several results. Once you have picked the correct person, you are actually redirected to the entry listed under his pseudonym, the name by which he was better known.

Why the Internet:

The A&E Biography site provides quick access to basic information on a person of historical significance. It covers more than 25,000 individuals, more people than any single print reference ever could.

Figure 3–13: Convert It! search result

6. *What is the equation for the chi^2 test?*

Answer:
$$f(\chi^2) = (\chi^2)^{\wedge(n/2 - 1)}\, e^{\wedge(-\chi^2/2)}\, 2^{\wedge(-n/2)}/r(n/2)$$

Site Used:
   Dave's Math Tables, available at: *www.sisweb.com/math/tables.htm*

Best Method (see Figure 3–12):
   Select Statistics, then Distributions, then chi^2-distributions.

Typical Pitfalls:
   Though this site does have a search function, it will not work for this question since you cannot input a superscripted number two. Searching on *chi2* will get no results; searching on *chi* will retrieve one result but it is not the one needed. Knowing that this

test is in the statistics category is necessary. If you did not know this, a quick reference interview should establish this fact.

Why the Internet:
The site is quick to load, organized by category, and searchable. The complete site can also be downloaded for the patron to take and view off-line.

7.   *I'm thinking of purchasing a plot of land. The old man who is selling it says that the size of the plot is 3 hectares. How many acres is that?*

Answer:
7.413 acres

Site Used:
Convert It! Available at *http://microimg.com/science/*

Best Method (see Figure 3–13):
Select area equivalents, enter *3* in the number box. Set *From:* to hectares. Set *To:* to acres. Click the conversion button.

Typical Pitfalls:
This one is straightforward. Sometimes people will get the *from* and *to* options backwards.

Why the Internet:
Almost any print volume that will assist you in answering this question will at best give you the necessary formula. This site will give you the answer.

8.   *What time is it?*

Answer:
I suppose it depends on what the clock says right now.

Site Used:
There is no good site for this question.

Best Method:
Look at your watch, the nearest clock on the wall, or the clock on your computer's screen.

Typical Pitfalls:
Following my directions and using the Internet to answer this question.

Figure 3–14: The cornerstone on the Nevada State Capital Building

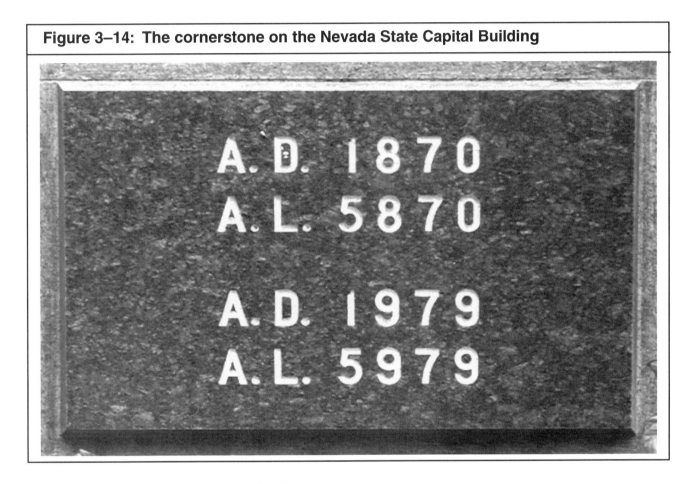

Why the Internet:

Once many librarians master the Internet to answer questions, they may turn to it automatically. Despite my instructions this is not a question you should ever use the Internet to answer. If a patron came up to your reference desk and asked you what time it was, would you say "wait a minute, let me use the Internet to look that up?" No. The Internet might be a useful resource to specify what time it is if the question were presented slightly differently. If the patron needed to know the "exact" time, or if he or she needed to know the time in another country, then the Internet may be of use. However, the question as stated does not need the Internet to be answered.

HOW TO CHOOSE THE BEST TYPE OF RESOURCE

Yes, that last one was a trick question, but it was one designed to make you think about when to choose one type of resource over another. If I had asked what time it is in Zimbabwe, then the Internet might have been appropriate. If you needed an online reference for the correct time to adjust your watch, then the Internet would be appropriate again. But for the question, as presented, the Internet is the wrong way to go. Let me share with you a story to further illustrate this point.

Sometimes the Internet is not specific enough and you need to consider other sources. A few years ago, my boss returned from a trip to Reno, the capital of Nevada. While walking by the state capitol building he had noticed a cornerstone (see Figure 3–14):

He wondered what calendar used the abbreviation "A.L.". Taking this as a personal challenge (as most great reference librarians would) I decided to find the answer for him. I spent almost half an hour on the Internet with all of the resources and search engines I had at my disposal basically wasting my time and getting nowhere fast. My boss came into my office and asked how it was going. I said not well, but had a sudden burst of inspiration and told him to give me five more minutes and then I would give up. He walked away giving me one last chance.

Five minutes later I went to his office and gave him the answer; A.L. is the Latin abbreviation for "In the year of light" and represents the Masonic calendar that starts in 4000 B.C.

What did I do to find the answer? The first thing I did was give up on the Internet and consider my resources. One of those resources was a two-volume set of books titled *The American Libraries Directory*. I looked up the Nevada State Library, called their reference desk, and gave the librarian on duty my question. She put me on hold for about two minutes and then gave me the answer.

Here's another story about the problem of relying too heavily on the Internet. One Sunday my home Internet connection had been down for four straight days. I was feeling a little frustrated at the whole thing by this time but was finding other things to do around the house. My wife, Denice, decided that she needed to go to a local store that we had not been to before. It was late in the afternoon and she was not sure how late the store would be open. She asked me to give the store a call and ask when it closed that day. She will never let me live down the first words out of my mouth. My answer "How can I look up their phone number? The Internet is down?"

Her response? "I don't know, the phone book?"

The moral of these stories: the Internet does not have all the answers and even when it does, it still might not be the best way to go about finding them. Before going to the Internet consider whether it is an appropriate way to answer your question.

READY REFERENCE RESOURCES

The following is a list of useful Internet resources to employ when answering ready reference questions.

Absolute Trivia (*www.absolutetrivia.com/*)
"The Totally Trivia Search Engine—More than 20,000 Facts—Updated Daily."

Acronym and Abbreviation Server (*www.ucc.ie/acronyms/acro.html*)
Search by acronym to see what that acronym means or by topic keyword to see what acronyms are related to that subject.

Air Traffic Control System Command Center (*www.fly.faa.gov/*)
"Real-time Airport Status page. Select an airport from the map or from the drop-down list to obtain the latest delay information."

Archive of Misheard Lyrics (*www.kissthisguy.com/*)
A listing of songs and their lyrics that have been misheard over the years. All of the listings are submitted by users of the site.

Atlapedia Online (*www.atlapedia.com/*)
"Contains full color physical and political maps as well as key facts and statistics on countries of the world."

Atomic Clock at the U.S. Naval Observatory (*http://tycho.usno.navy.mil/what.html*)
If you need to know the exact time here is the Web site you need.

Bartlett's Familiar Quotations (*www.cc.columbia.edu/acis/bartleby/bartlett/*)
"This tenth edition of 1919 contains over 11,000 searchable quotations and was the first new edition of John Bartlett's corpus to be published after his death in 1905."

Biography.com (*www.biography.com/*)
Web site for the Biography series on the Arts and Entertainment cable network. This database indexes over 25,000 famous persons and personalities. Brief biographies can be retrieved along with links to related Web sites.

Body Mass Index Calculator (*www.thriveonline.com/weight/tools/bmi.html*)
"To find your BMI, type in your height and weight, then click on 'calculate.'"

Book-A-Minute (*http://rinkworks.com/bookaminute/*)
Contains very humorous yet highly accurate synopses of classic literature.

Bureau of the Census (*www.census.gov/*)
The central repository for all U.S. Census data, updated with the 2000 data in the Spring of 2001.

Calculator.com (*www.calculator.com/*)
"Free access to online calculators to help you solve problems and answer questions in the home, office, and school. There are calculators for finance, business, and science. There are ones for cooking, hobbies, and health. Some solve problems, some satisfy curiosity, and some are just for fun. All put the answer easily within your reach."

Cambridge Dictionaries Online (*www.cup.cam.ac.uk/esl/dictionary/*)
Access to the *Cambridge International Dictionary of English*, the *Cambridge Dictionary of American English*, the *Cambridge International Dictionary of Idioms*, and the *Cambridge International Dictionary of Phrasal Verbs*.

Canadian Postal Code Lookup Service (*www.westminster.cA/cdnlook.htm*)
"Enter the full Street Address, City, and Province for the Canadian mailing address you want to find."

Clothing Conversion (*www.houseoftravel.com/clothing.htm*)
Convert American, British, and continental clothing sizes for men, women, and children.

Convert It! (*http://microimg.com/science/*)
Convert measurements in the following categories: acceleration, area, energy/work, power, length, mass, metrology, pressure, temperature, U.S. fluid or liquid, velocity, and volume/capacity.

Crossword Solver (sorta) (*www.ojohaven.com/fun/crossword.html*)
"This engine finds only single English words, not phrases, names, or proper nouns (yet), and it only supports words up to 10 letters long."

Currency Converter (*www3.travelocity.com/converter/*)
Convert 75 different world currencies. The answer will be given in the direction asked for and in reverse in the case of user input error.

Date and Time Gateway (*www.bsdi.com/date/*)
Find the current time in major cities around the world. Data is accessed through an alphabetical listing of cities by country.

EarthMaps (*www.earthmaps.com/*)
Create a map of any location based on place name, zip code, street address, area code and exchange, or latitude/longitude. Maps can be resized, panned, rescaled, and zoomed.

FedStats (*www.fedstats.gov/*)
"The gateway to statistics from over 100 U.S. Federal agencies."

Flight Tracking (*www.thetrip.com/usertools/flighttracking/*)
"Find out the current status of any flights between major cities within the United States." I especially like this one because you can get a real-time graphical representation of where the plane is.

Geographic Names Information System (*http://mapping.usgs.gov/www/gnis/*)
"Developed by the U.S. Geographic Survey (USGS) in cooperation with the U.S. Board on Geographic Names (BGN), contains information about almost 2 million physical and cultural geographic features in the United States. The federally recognized name of each feature described in the data base is identified, and references are made to a feature's location by state, county, and geographic coordinates."

Getty Thesaurus of Geographic Names (*http://shiva.pub.getty.edu/tgn_browser/*)
"The TGN is a structured vocabulary containing around 1,000,000 names and other information about places. The TGN includes all continents and nations of the modern political world, as well as historical places. It includes physical features and administrative entities, such as cities and nations. The emphasis in TGN is on places important for art and architecture."

Gist-In-Time (*www.teletranslator.com:8080/*)
Translate Web pages into English, Spanish, French, German, Japanese, Italian, and Portuguese. The site interface is available in English, Japanese, French, and German.

How Far Is It? (*www.indo.com/distance/*)
"This service uses data from the U.S. Census and a supplementary list of cities around the world to find the latitude and longitude of two places, and then calculates the distance between them (as the crow flies). It also provides a map showing the two places, using the Xerox PARC Map Server."

Inflation Calculators (*www.jsc.nasa.gov/bu2/inflate.html*)
Contains five different inflation calculators based on the Consumer Price Index (CPI), the Employment Cost Index, the Gross Domestic Product Index (GDP), the International Price Index, and the Producer Price Index.

Internet Dictionary Project (*www.june29.com/IDP/IDPsearch.html*)
Translate words between from English to French, German, Italian, Latin, Portuguese, or Spanish quickly and simply. Translation from those languages to English is also available.

Internet Movie Database (*www.imdb.com/*)
"We catalog all sorts of information on over 200,000 movie & TV titles plus even more on over 400,000 actors and actresses, nearly 40,000 directors and hundreds of thousands of other people who help make magic on the big and small screens. Then we take all that information, organize it into a cool structure, and make it possible for you to easily search and browse through it."

Kiplinger's Financial Calculators (*www.kiplinger.com/tools/*)
Over 60 different financial calculators are accessible from this one page. Topics include inventing, managing, spending, credit, stocks, cars, college, insurance, and taxes.

MapQuest (*www.mapquest.com/*)
Find your way from one point to another. Print out your route or download it to your personal digital assistant (PDA).

Math Tables (*www.sisweb.com/math/tables.htm*)
Need to find that math formula you haven't used since high school? Check here. Contains formulas for the following categories: General Math, Algebra, Geometry, Linear Algebra, Discrete Math, Statistics, Calculus, and others.

Metric and English Conversion Utility (*www.psinvention.com/zoetic/convert.htm*)
Convert English and metric measurements easily.

National Population Clock (*www.census.gov/cgi-bin/popclock/*)
The most current estimated population of the United States from the U.S. Census Bureau.

The Old Farmer's Almanac (*www.almanac.com/*)
Your complete guide to the best times to plant in the U.S.

OnHealth Drug Database (*http://onhealth.webmd.com/conditions/resource/pharmacy/index.asp*)
"Clear, objective information about thousands of prescription and over-the-counter medications. Find out how to take your medicine and whether it may cause side effects or adverse interactions with other drugs. Look up a medication by its brand name or its generic name. If you're taking more than one medication, use another tool to check for unwanted drug interactions."

Relationship Chart (*www.grl.com/grl/relationship.html*)
Figure out just how you are related to that Fifth Cousin Twice Removed.

Reverse Phone Look Up (*www.555-1212.com/index.jsp#SearchReverse*)
"Get the listing for a phone number in the U.S. or Canada."

Rhyme Zone (*www.rhymezone.com/*)
Type in a word to find its rhymes, homophones, synonyms, similar words, and other information.

Roget's Thesaurus of English Words and Phrases (*www.thesaurus.com/*)
Your online thesaurus.

SongFile (*www.songfile.com/index_2.html*)
"Search the database of over 2 million songs and view more than 62,000 lyrics from our rapidly growing database of more than 130,000 songs."

Symbols of the World (*www.symbols.com/*)
"SYMBOLS.com contains more than 2,500 Western signs, arranged into 54 groups according to their graphic characteristics. In 1,600 articles their histories, uses, and meanings are thoroughly discussed. The signs range from ideograms carved in mammoth teeth by Cro-Magnon men, to hobo signs and subway graffiti."

UK Postcodes On-line (*http://pol.royalmail.com/PF.asp*)
Enter an address using a combination of premises, street, and town to find the correct postcode.

U.S. Gazetteer (*www.census.gov/cgi-bin/gazetteer/*)
"This gazetteer is used to identify places to view with the Tiger Map Server and obtain census data from the 1990 Census Lookup server. You can search for places, counties, or MCDs by entering the name and state abbreviation (optional), or 5-digit zip code."

U.S. Post Office's Online Postage Rate Calculator (*http://postcalc.usps.gov/*)
Retrieve the correct postage amount to send your letter or package based on how quickly you would like it to get there and what additional services you require. Both domestic and international calculators are available.

U.S. Statistical Abstract (*www.census.gov/stat_abstract/*)
"As the National Data Book it contains a collection of statistics on social and economic conditions in the United States. Selected international data are also included. The Abstract is also your Guide to Sources of other data from the Census Bureau, other Federal agencies, and private organizations. A special feature of this edition is a new section, 20th Century Statistics, which presents data beginning in 1900 where available on a broad range of subjects such as population, education, income and labor force."

U.S. Zip Code Lookup (*www.westminster.ca/usalook.htm*)
"Enter the full Street Address, City, and State for the American mailing address you want to find. If you have an existing Zip Code, enter it as well, since it can be used to resolve ambiguities in the address."

Who Is That (*www.who-is-that.com/*)
"The web site where we lay down the smack on contemporary character actors. We've got new features about the character actors you see all the time in movies and wonder, 'who is that?'"

Xerox PARC Map Viewer (*http://mapweb.parc.xerox.com/map*)
"The Xerox PARC Map Viewer is a World-Wide Web HTTP server that accepts requests for a World or USA map and returns an HTML document including an image of the requested map. Each map image is created on demand from a geographic database. Selecting on the map image requests a new map zoomed in on the selected point. Links embedded in the HTML document control other map rendering options."

Your Nation (*www.your-nation.com/*)
At this site you can "compare statistics for any two countries of your choice, rank countries by a statistic of your choice, and display a summary of a country."

4 COMPARING SEARCH ENGINES AND DIRECTORIES

There are two major types of finding aids on the Internet today: search engines and directories. Many users are unaware that there are significant differences between them.

SEARCH ENGINES

Search engines include such sites as AltaVista, HotBot, Google, Northern Light, and Lycos. (Notice I did not list Yahoo!. That is a directory, as I'll show later.) Boiled down to the core, search engines can be defined as "an automated index of words on Web pages." [Dummies Daily: Internet Search, 10 February 2000. Available at *www.dummiesdaily.com/*]

Let me explain that a little further:

> **Automated index:** Search engines use programs to automatically index pages. These programs are officially called "user agents" but are more commonly known as "bots" or "spiders." They are given a starting point (a URL) and let loose. The bot will then go to that page, index it, find links to other pages, and follow those links, indexing any new pages it finds. Whenever it is done indexing a page it will send the indexed data back to the search engine's database, in what I like to call "the golden pile."

> **Words on Web pages:** When a bot comes to a page it looks at the HTML code behind the page. It finds all of the individual words on that page (including words that may not be usually displayed to a user, such as metadata) and makes a note of them. When that data is sent back to the search engine's pile, a note is made that word X appears on a particular page. When you go to a search engine and search on a keyword, the search engine will return a list of every page it knows about in which that word appears.

DIRECTORIES

Directories include such sites and Yahoo!, FindLaw, Cyndi's List, and The Scout Report. Directories can best be defined as "human-created categorized listings of Web sites." [Dummies Daily: Internet Search, 10 February 2000. Available at *www.dummiesdaily.com/*]

Here's the breakdown:

Human-created: A directory's creation does not rely on software to do the finding. People who find the sites (or gather submissions by other people) and organize them into categories do most of the work.

Categorized: Directories will organize their listings into major categories and then, in many cases, into subcategories as appropriate. You do not have to search a directory to find the site you are looking for. A well-organized directory will allow you to find what you are looking for by browsing.

Listing of Web sites: Directories do not index every page of every site they find. When you do find what you are looking for in a directory, you will usually be pointed to the first page of a whole site. Unlike search engines, directories will rarely list more than one page from a site.

POINTING OUT THE SIMILARITIES AND DIFFERENCES

You may be thinking, "But wait, you can keyword search Yahoo!, and HotBot has browsable categories!" That is true, but the addition of categories does not make a search engine a directory; neither does keyword searching make a directory a search engine. What you need to do is take a look at the core technology behind the site.

Let me use Google as an example. When you reach the Google homepage you are presented with a search box and not much else. When you click the search button you are presented with a list of pages that contain your search terms. (In fact, Google shows you the context of your keywords by giving you back some of the page's text with your words in bold.) Google also often returns more than one page from the same site, indenting the results that are from the same site as the previous result. Google is a search engine.

Yahoo!, however, is a directory. You have the ability to pick from one of several major categories (computers, art, history, etc.). Once you have picked a major category, you are presented with subcategories. Once you reach the specific topic for which you are searching, you can pick from a list of sites that deal with that topic. You will rarely see more than one item listed with the same domain name (at the same site).

The keyword searching available at the Yahoo! site was added once Yahoo!'s directory was large enough to justify it. Originally, there was no keyword searching at Yahoo!. Search engines that have added directories in the past year or two (HotBot, AltaVista) have done so because many users prefer that method and the services wish to attract more users. One other significant point about those categories is that they are not complete. In HotBot's photography category, you will not find every site that the HotBot service knows about. You will only have access to sites that have been selected from the larger HotBot database by HotBot's employees.

TYPES OF SEARCH ENGINES

Search engines can be broken down into three major types: general, subject specific, and meta. Let's discuss in more detail each type—its benefits and its drawbacks.

GENERAL

General search engines are the ones that get the most press, have been around the longest, and are therefore the most familiar to most Internet users. General search engines index any and every page that they can. In the early days of search engines, a few even claimed to index over 90 percent (if not all) of the pages on the Web. (No search engine claims that today.) The general category includes HotBot, AltaVista, Google, Lycos, and Excite. General search engines are popular for the breadth in all subjects and topics. Unfortunately they also suffer due to their size, often returning more results than most users could ever browse.

Two Ohio librarians sought to verify the accuracy of information retrieved using the AltaVista search engine. They used a sample of 60 patron-generated reference questions, and looked at only the first 20 results returned by AltaVista. Their searches frequently had to be rephrased to retrieve relevant results. Of the results returned, they found that 12 percent were dead links. Over 60 percent of the remaining pages did not provide any answer to the question, and 8 percent provided a wrong or mostly wrong answer. However, 27 percent of pages provided correct or mostly correct results, leading the researchers to conclude that getting a correct answer to a query was three times as likely as finding an incorrect answer, although finding no answer was far more likely than either possibility.

Source: Tschera Harkness Connell and Jennifer E. Tipple. "Testing the Accuracy of Information on the World Wide Web Using the AltaVista Search Engine." *Reference and User Services Quarterly*, 38(4): Summer 1999. p. 360.

SUBJECT SPECIFIC

Subject specific search engines work just like general ones but are more limited in scope. These search engines may focus on a particular subject, topic, or geographic area. The subject specific category includes GovBot, EuroSearch, and The James Kirk Search Engine. (I'll give you one guess as to what type of site the latter indexes.) Subject specific search engines work well in many cases due to a narrower focus than general search engines have. Their problem lies in the fact that many subjects do not have this type of service available.

META

Meta search engines have been becoming more and more popular of late. Meta search engines distinguish themselves by what they do not have: their own databases of indexed pages. Meta search engines allow you to enter keywords that are then sent off to other search engines (general ones, subject specific ones, or a combination of both. In many cases Yahoo! is included since it is the most comprehensive directory available.) The meta category includes Inference Find, MetaCrawler, and Copernic. Meta search engines allow users to access the benefits of multiple databases of indexed pages in an easy-to-use interface. What metas lack is the ability to answer the complex queries that the serious researcher needs to know.

TYPES OF DIRECTORIES

GENERAL

General directories are similar to general search engines in that they attempt to cover any and all subjects and topics. There are very few sites that fall into the general category. Yahoo! is the one almost everyone can name. There are others, such as CyberDewey and ZenSearch, but they do not yet compare to the breadth of coverage that Yahoo! has. General directories give the average user the ability to browse and find what they are looking for without having to learn a search syntax. Unlike general search engines, their breadth, in pure number of sites, is very limited.

SUBJECT SPECIFIC

Subject specific directories abound on the Internet today. Anyone with a subject knowledge and a little bit of HTML can put together a subject specific directory. Cyndi's List is a great example. This site lists tens of thousands of genealogy sites. I also run a subject specific directory, the WWW Library Directory, a geographically based directory of more than 7,000 library Web sites from around the world. Subject specific directories benefit from their creator's knowledge in the subject but can be problematic when that creator fails to keep the material up-to-date as can happen to many a great site.

REVIEWED

Reviewed directories can be either general or subject specific but add one additional feature. Humans not only select the sites and categorize them but take the additional time to evaluate each site and post a review (usually short) along with the listing itself. Sites in this category include The Scout Report, Argus Clearinghouse (though Argus rates sites instead of actually reviewing them), and Brittannica.com. These sites separate the wheat from the chaff, listing only sites of merit and specifically not listing sites that the reviewer does not consider of significant use. These directories usually have the smallest database of sites of all the other types of directories and search engines.

HOW GENERAL SEARCH ENGINES FAIL

The last major study of search engine index sizes determined that only about 1/3 of the Web's estimated 800 million pages are actually indexed by search engines. Ever think about what pages aren't being indexed? Certain Web pages, and whole sites, are not being indexed for a variety of reasons. These pages (and sites) can be broken down into the following categories:

- **Database/Dynamic**
  Any Web page that is created on the fly by querying a database of information through user input or pages that are generated for a particular user based on preferences set by that user. Typically pages end in .asp, .cgi, or contain question marks in the URL. Example: You are asked for your name and zip code. From then on whenever you visit the site it welcomes you by name and displays information relevant to your location.
- **Constantly updated**
  Sites and pages that are different almost every time you visit them or are changed at least once a day. There is no possible way for any search engine to keep up. Example: Search on a current event or person in the news. You will not find New York Times articles as hits unless you are specifically using the NYT search function on their site.
- **Frames**
  Because of how "frameset" documents are coded, almost all information presented in frames is not indexed. The author of a frames-based site can code a "noframes" version of the site that would allow search engines in, but might not do it either through ignorance or apathy. Unfortunately, by not doing this, the author is also preventing users with accessibility issues from accessing the information. The following example (see Figure 4–1) is a frames-based site. Note that only lines 12–16 and 31–36 will be indexed.
- **Non-Latin character sets**
  Sites that are in foreign languages not generally supported by the ASCII character set. Examples include Chinese, Thai, and Hebrew.

    The example in Figure 4–2 shows a version of the Google homepage in Chinese. Unfortunately, the browser used does not support the "Big5" Chinese character set

Figure 4–1: The HTML code for HyperHistory

```
12  <META Name="description" Content="World History : HyperHistory Online navigates
13   through 3 000 years of World History with links to important persons of
14  world historical importance; civilization timelines; events and facts; and
15  historical maps">
16  <META Name="keywords" Content="World History, history, Free, Information, Online, Buy Chart, mille
17  <INPUT TYPE=hidden VALUE="world history, history, Free, Information, Online, Buy Chart, millennium
18  </HEAD>
19  <frameset rows=*,42 border=no>
20          <frameset cols=60,*,190>
21                  <frame src=navbar.html name=frame_menu noresize MARGINWIDTH=1 MARGINHEIGHT=4 scrolling
22                  <frame src=main.html name=frame_landscape MARGINWIDTH=0 MARGINHEIGHT=0>
23                  <frame src=text.html name=frame_text noresize MARGINWIDTH=4 MARGINHEIGHT=3>
24          </frameset>
25
26          <frameset cols=*>
27                  <frame src=index.html name=index_menu noresize MARGINWIDTH=0 MARGINHEIGHT=0 scrolling=
28          </frameset>
29  </frameset>
30  <noframeset>
31  World History : 3,000 years of world history timelines<BR>
32  HyperHistory presents 3000 years of world history with a combination of colorful graphics,
33  lifelines, timelines, and maps. Over a thousand files are interconnected throughout the website.
34  The site contains over 10 MB of images and text files, but individual gif files are kept small
35  enough to allow for a quick display.<P>World History: HyperHistory Online can only be seen
36  with a frame capable browser</noframeset>
```

Figure 4–2: The Chinese version of Google

Figure 4–3: The source code for the Chinese version of Google

```
39  &para;i&para;&yen;&middot;j&acute;M</a><br>
40   <a href="/preferences?hl=zh-TW">
41  &uml;&Iuml;&yen;&Icirc;&deg;&frac34;&brvbar;n</a></font></td>
42  </tr>
43
44  <tr>
45  <td colspan="3" align="center"><font size="-1" face=""><input
46  type="radio" name="lr" value="">
47  &middot;j&acute;M&copy;&Ograve;&brvbar;&sup3;&ordm;&ocirc;&macr;&cedil;
48  <input type="radio" name="lr" value="lang_zh-TW" checked>
49  &middot;j&acute;M&curren;&curren;&curren;&aring;(&Aacute;c&Aring;&eacute;)&ordm;
50  &ocirc;&shy;&para;</font></td>
51  </tr>
52  </table>
53  </form>
54
55  <br>
56  <br>
57  <p><font size="-1"><a href="/intl/zh-TW/about.html">
58  Google&sect;&sup1;&yen;&thorn;&curren;&acirc;&yen;U</a> - <a
59  href="/intl/zh-TW/help.html">
60  &middot;j&acute;M&laquo;&Oslash;&Auml;&sup3;</a> - <a href=
61  "http://www.google.com/en">Google in English</a></font></p>
62
63  <p><font size="-1"><font size="-2" color="#999999">&copy;2001
64  Google</font></font></p>
65  </center>
```

that is being used to write this page. This is exactly how a search engine would read this page if it were not preprogrammed to understand Chinese characters, which many search engines are not.

Now look at the source code for Google's Chinese version (see Figure 4–3). Since a different character set is being used, there is not much to index.

• **Restricted**
A Web page, or whole site for that matter, can be restricted to prevent certain users from accessing it. How this is accomplished is up to the author of the site but as long as a person has a reason, restriction is easily accomplished.

The main method by which to accomplish the blocking of a site is password protection. Once a password has been established, only users with the correct password (and usually an associated user-name) may access that information. Since the search engine's software does not have the password, it cannot index the associated pages.

For example, I offer some online classes through BCR. In order to access the online class material you must regis-

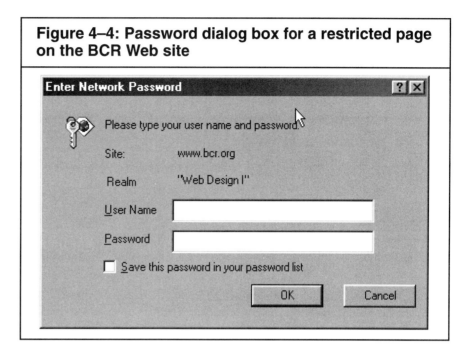

Figure 4–4: Password dialog box for a restricted page on the BCR Web site

ter for the class and receive the access username and password from me. Those who sign up for the class are allowed access. Whenever they attempt to access the class material they are presented with a browser window asking them for the appropriate user-name and password (see Figure 4–4).

Another way a site's author may restrict access is through a registration process. For example, in order to access the Johns Hopkins Antibiotic Guide you are first asked to register (see Figure 4–5). There may not be a password associated with registration. Instead, the site may set a cookie on your computer that identifies you as a registered user and allows you access. Since the search engine software is not equipped to register, it cannot gain access to the material in order to index it.

- **Blocked**
  It is possible for a Web master to block a search engine from indexing part of its site, or even keep search engines out completely using a "robots.txt" file or by password protecting a page or site.

  Examples: Figure 4–6 shows the robots.txt file from OCLC. As displayed, all search engine robots (User-agent: *) are being kept out of many of the site's directories. From reading the list many of them are understandable. All "cgi-" directories contain scripts that assist the user in interact-

Figure 4–5: Registration page of the Johns Hopkins Division of Infectious Diseases Web site

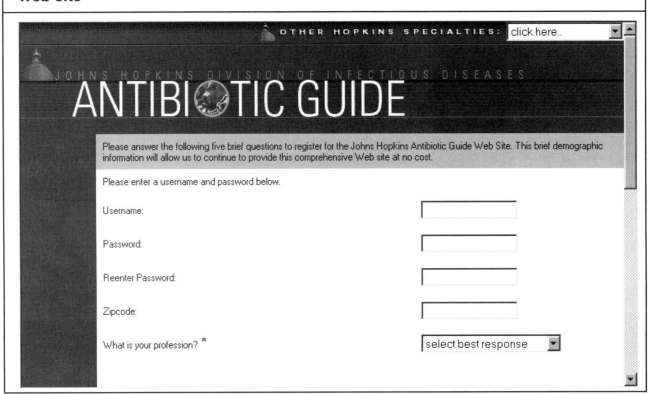

Figure 4–6: OCLC's robots.txt file

```
User-agent: *
Disallow: /cgi-prism
Disallow: /cgi-bin
Disallow: /cgi-oclc
Disallow: /cgi-fred
Disallow: /oclc/forms
Disallow: /network
Disallow: /cic
Disallow: /test
Disallow: /RCS
Disallow: /secure
Disallow: /test
Disallow: /dist
Disallow: /oclc/fp/mrdui
Disallow: /secure/scenarios
Disallow: /~
```

Figure 4–7: Meta data used to prevent indexing of a page and its subpages

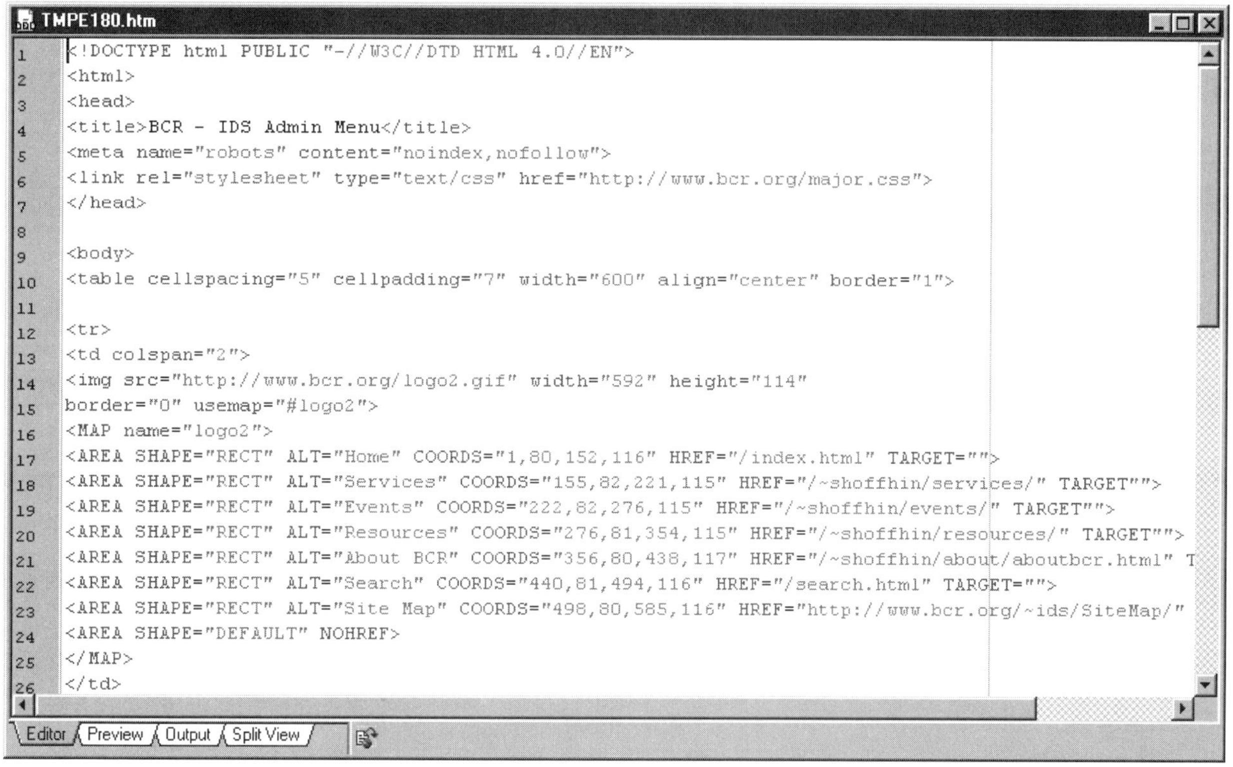

```
TMPE180.htm

1   <!DOCTYPE html PUBLIC "-//W3C//DTD HTML 4.0//EN">
2   <html>
3   <head>
4   <title>BCR - IDS Admin Menu</title>
5   <meta name="robots" content="noindex,nofollow">
6   <link rel="stylesheet" type="text/css" href="http://www.bcr.org/major.css">
7   </head>
8
9   <body>
10  <table cellspacing="5" cellpadding="7" width="600" align="center" border="1">
11
12  <tr>
13  <td colspan="2">
14  <img src="http://www.bcr.org/logo2.gif" width="592" height="114"
15  border="0" usemap="#logo2">
16  <MAP name="logo2">
17  <AREA SHAPE="RECT" ALT="Home" COORDS="1,80,152,116" HREF="/index.html" TARGET="">
18  <AREA SHAPE="RECT" ALT="Services" COORDS="155,82,221,115" HREF="/~shoffhin/services/" TARGET="">
19  <AREA SHAPE="RECT" ALT="Events" COORDS="222,82,276,115" HREF="/~shoffhin/events/" TARGET="">
20  <AREA SHAPE="RECT" ALT="Resources" COORDS="276,81,354,115" HREF="/~shoffhin/resources/" TARGET="">
21  <AREA SHAPE="RECT" ALT="About BCR" COORDS="356,80,438,117" HREF="/~shoffhin/about/aboutbcr.html" T
22  <AREA SHAPE="RECT" ALT="Search" COORDS="440,81,494,116" HREF="/search.html" TARGET="">
23  <AREA SHAPE="RECT" ALT="Site Map" COORDS="498,80,585,116" HREF="http://www.bcr.org/~ids/SiteMap/"
24  <AREA SHAPE="DEFAULT" NOHREF>
25  </MAP>
26  </td>
```

Editor / Preview / Output / Split View /

ing with the site, "test" directories contain pages not yet ready for general access, and "secure" directories are also not for general access. As for the other directories, I'm sure OCLC has their reasons for keeping search engines out.

If the author of a site has a much smaller section of their site that they would like to prevent from being indexed, the author may also take advantage of meta data in the document's HTML code. Notice in line five of Figure 4–7 how the author employed meta data to prevent indexing of a page and its subpages.

In the above example, the author is indicating to any search engine software that may encounter this page that the document is not to be indexed (noindex) and that it should not follow any links in this page in an attempt to index those documents (nofollow).

• **Unknown**
The site is unknown just to the search engine. This always sounds like a cop-out to me but it is a legitimate category.

Let me explain the two methods a search engine uses to find pages to index.

In the first method, the author of the site announces to the search engine that the page(s) exist. The author fills out an online form that includes the starting URL for the site. This information is submitted to the search engine's spider for eventual indexing. There are many services available that will complete these announcements for a fee.

The other method is through serendipity. Whenever a spider indexes a page, it makes a note of all the links it finds on that page. When it is done with that page it will move on to the other pages through the links it found. This is why, through the submission of only one URL, a spider will index a whole site. This can also lead the spider to sites that had not been directly announced to it.

A page can be "unknown" if it does not fall into one of the above two categories. For example: I create a site, I tell only a few close friends, no other pages link to it, and I don't tell a search engine it exists.

- **Yet to be indexed**

This category was recently suggested to me by one of my workshop attendees in Jackson, Wyoming. He asked me "what about pages that are in indexing limbo?" This was an interesting question.

Through a little discussion we came up with the "yet to be indexed" category. Pages that fit into this category fit into the following scenario: the author has announced the page to a search engine but the spider has yet to get to the page for indexing.

I felt this was a stretch, but he then reminded me that most search engines have a 48-hour to two-week lag time between a page having been announced to them and when their spider actually gets to indexing the page due to the service's immense backlog. Once that time period starts measuring in weeks, there can be a significant number of pages at any one moment that are neither known or unknown, but in indexing limbo.

HOW SUBJECT SPECIFIC RESOURCES FILL THE GAP

In each of the cases listed in the previous section, How General Search Engines Fail, I did not mean to give you the impression that there is no way to find the information. The point was that big general search engines such as AltaVista, HotBot, and Google couldn't find this information.

There is a name for the information that is contained in all of those sites that cannot be found using general search engines: The Invisible Web. I do not like this term. Invisible things are generally difficult to find. But difficult does not necessarily mean impossible. The use of the term 'invisible' in describing this type of information should not be read to mean that the information cannot be found at all. What most searchers do not realize and need to learn is that there may be other ways to find this information. In most cases this is where subject specific resources (both directories and search engines) can assist you in finding the information you are looking for.

Let's take a look at those eight categories again and see how subject specific resources may help.

- **Database/Dynamic**
  In this case the search engine of the specific site in question will be your only solution. In order to search the catalog of products at Amazon.com you must use their search engine. Services like Google will not do you any good.
- **Constantly Updated**
  Like database-based and dynamic sites, the solution is the search engine at the particular site. The best way to find stories from CNN is to use the CNN.com search engine.
- **Frames**
  There is no real alternative to this one since it depends on the author of the site to code it properly for searching. The only possibility is if the author has included a search engine within the site as with the previous two categories. It has been my experience, however, that this does not occur as often as most would like.
- **Non-Latin character sets**
  In this case you need to find first a search engine or directory that is specifically geared for indexing material in that character set. Many of the major search engines and di-

rectories of today do have geographically specific services, such as Yahoo! Japan at *www.yahoo.co.jp/*. Once you have found one of these services you must also be sure that you have the correct software and/or hardware installed on your computer so as to be able to display that language properly. Finally you, or your patron, must be able to read that language.

- **Restricted**
  With this one you are out of luck unless you can ask and receive permission to enter the site. Once you have been able to do that, a site specific search engine will allow you to find the information you need.

- **Blocked**
  Most sites that block are not blocking everything. Try another search engine or a directory. You might have better luck with a directory since it is run by humans and will not blindly follow exclusion instructions as a search engine's software will.

- **Unknown**
  Here is another case where you may have better luck with a subject specific directory than with a subject specific search engine. Since this type of search engine has the same technical limitations as a general one, a site that falls into the unknown category will stay there. Once you get humans involved—as with a directory—they are more likely to find such a site through personal contacts instead of the more software-based searching methods.

- **Yet to be indexed**
  A page that falls into this category is similar to an unknown page but has the benefit of intent on the part of the author. It has been my experience that listings make it into subject specific directories much quicker than into any type of search engine or general directory. As someone who runs a subject specific directory myself, I know that once I have been informed of a new site I can usually get it into the directory within 24 hours, though sometimes it take a little longer. Most search engines have a turn-around time measured in days if not weeks.

5 CREATING A COMPLEX REFERENCE STRATEGY

Your reference collection will sometimes not work for more complex reference questions. These types of questions need a little more analysis before an answer can be presented. In these cases you will end up going to the regular nonfiction collection. In most cases you will not know this larger portion of your collection nearly as well as your regular reference collection, which rules out the two-step strategy I presented earlier. How must the strategy be modified to handle this situation?

EVALUATING YOUR PRINT STRATEGY

This part of my live class is always more challenging for me to teach. My recommended strategies for ready reference, showed you how to use the Internet successfully by trying a new method, my advice for answering complex reference situations using the Internet are not as clear-cut.

What I will be suggesting in this section is an alternative that you should consider when, or in some cases before, failure occurs with your current complex reference strategy.

Let me present you with the following question: Why was the murder of Francis Scott Key's son historically significant? I find this to be an extraordinary question since most people in the United States are completely unaware that Francis Scott Key's son was murdered, or that he even had a son.

How would you tackle this question? This is where things get difficult for me because you may have answered, "Look up Francis Scott Key in the encyclopedia." For argument's sake, let us assume that the encyclopedia does say that his son was murdered but goes no further than that.

Having ruled out the ready reference collection you determine that you will need to hunt in the general collection. Depending on the size of your collection, this may or may not be a daunting task. The answer to this interesting question will be one of our complex reference exercises later in this chapter. For now let's consider how we might start trying to answer a question like this. Let me suggest that you would probably pursue the following strategy:

1. Go to the OPAC
2. Type in *francis scott key* or maybe *american history*
3. Retrieve a list of results
4. Make a note of the general location of those results via the call numbers
5. Go to that shelf, or shelves, depending on the size of the collection
6. Browse the shelf
7. Pick a book
8. Search the book, usually via the index, for the answer

Admittedly you may need to select another book if the first does not have the answer. What you generally will not need to do is go to another area of the collection or even another OPAC. (You may go to an ILL system if you were unsuccessful in finding an answer.)

EVALUATING YOUR CURRENT INTERNET STRATEGY

Now, how would you treat this question if you had to use the Internet? From my experience, you would probably do something like this:

1. Go to your favorite search engine
2. Type in *francis scott key son murder*
3. Wait for results
4. Retrieve approximately 1,699,453 results
5. Click on the first result
6. Wait for document to load
7. Find answer

This list, at first glance, is shorter than the print one. But you're forgetting that this is not a perfect world. It's the Internet. Typically, that last step—Find answer—does not happen that quickly. Replace "Find answer" with the following:

1. Don't find answer
2. Back up
3. Click on another result
4. Wait for document to load

5. Don't find answer
6. Repeat until frustrated
7. Try new keywords
8. Wait some more
9. Pick some more results
10. Still don't find answer
11. Try another search engine
12. Give up and go to the print collection

CREATING AN EFFECTIVE INTERNET STRATEGY

I am not here to say that the above Internet strategy will not work. Unlike when we dealt with ready reference questions where I said not to do it the way you had been doing it, here I am offering an effective alternative that you can use if your current strategy fails. Eventually, once you have enough experience with complex searching, you will be able to tell when the first strategy is likely to fail before you even try it.

Let us compare print versus the Internet:

Print Strategy

1. Go to the OPAC
2. Type in the subject of the question
3. Retrieve a list of results relating to that subject
4. Make a note of the general location of that subject via the call numbers
5. Go to that shelf, or shelves, depending on the size of the collection
6. Browse the shelf
7. Pick a book
8. Search the book, via the index, for the answer

Internet Strategy

1. Go to your favorite search engine
2. Type in keywords
3. Wait for results
4. Retrieve approximately 1,699,453 results
5. Click on the first result
6. Wait for document to load
7. Find answer

One thing you can do to immediately improve your Internet results is to read the titles and descriptions of *all* the hits found on the first page of results *before* clicking on one of them. I am so surprised when I ask a roomful of librarians how many do this. Usually only about one out of ten says they do. Most just start reading down the list and click on the first one that looks good. But what if the next hit is better?

Ordinarily you should never go beyond the first two pages of results (20 to 25 hits). What do you think the odds are that the site you're looking for can be found at hit number 8,764 or even 372? Add to that how much time it took you to get there. You are much better off submitting a new search.

As I said earlier, it does look like the Internet is shorter, which in fact it can be, but experience tells us that this is not always the case.

To see the distinction between the two strategies, ask yourself the following question: At which step in the strategies did we start to treat Internet and print resources differently?

The answer is the second step, "Type in keywords."

With print we went looking for something that had the answer. With the Internet we immediately went for the answer. Why do we insist that all we need to do is type in a few keywords and get an answer back? You would not consider looking for the answer to a reference question with your OPAC, so why do you do it with the Internet?

The reason going right for the answer often fails is that the answer may be on one of the Web pages we discussed earlier—the ones that major search engines cannot index. If this is the case, you will never find what you're looking for no matter how accurate your keywords are or how complex your search statement may be.

What I am suggesting is that you treat the Internet as you would your OPAC and look for a site that would have the answer. Let me share the following story with you that will illustrate my point.

Whenever I give the live version of this class to a roomful of librarians, one of them always comes up to me during one of the breaks or over lunch, gives me a sheepish look, and starts a question with "I had this patron the other day whose question I could not find an answer to." They then proceed to unintentionally challenge me to find how to answer the question that stumped them. This is a challenge I love! So far I'm running at about a 90 percent success rate.

One librarian had a question for herself, not a patron. She told me that she had the base to a GE electric blender from the 1950s. The base of the blender worked fine but she was missing the bowl that attached to it, rendering it useless. She wanted me to find the bowl to her blender.

I thought about this question for a moment and quickly determined that going to some search engine like Google or AltaVista and searching on keywords like "GE," "blender," and "bowl" was going to be a complete waste of time. Instead I thought, What is this question about? What would I type into an OPAC? I really do not like to admit this, and did not to the woman, but I came up with the subject of "old junk." I realize that this was not exactly respectful nor something that you would ever type into an OPAC, but it was the best I could come up with at the time.

Can you guess where I decided the best place to find old junk on the Internet was? eBay.

I went over to eBay (think of it like a book on the shelf in your print collection) and did a search for *ge blender electric old*. Within seconds I had found a listing for a complete GE electric blender, bowl, and base, exactly matching what the woman wanted.

The above example shows the process that you can apply to these types of questions. I was able to determine that the old strategy was not going to work. Then, since I had the Internet experience, I was able to do the subject search right in my head (the OPAC) coming up with a specific site (the shelf) that dealt with my topic. From there I did a subject specific search (browsing the books on the shelf) to find exactly what I was looking for.

Here are a few other examples of how this strategy works in real-life situations.

Joy Hungenberg of the Eaton Public Library in Colorado told me about a patron who came in with the wrapper from a Danish cough drop. The patron reported that the place she had been purchasing them could no longer afford the overseas shipping and would no longer be carrying them. She wanted to know where else she could purchase them, showing Joy a wrapper from one of the cough drops. Joy started out by searching for the name of the product and ending up in sites that listed pharmaceutical companies in Denmark. Quickly realizing that neither she nor the patron spoke or read Danish, this strategy was getting her nowhere. Joy then took a step back and thought about the larger subject that this question fell under. Joy determined that this woman would have to "purchase" these from a company and the fact that the cough drop in question was of Danish origin was irrelevant. Joy ended up looking for online pharmacies and did find one that carried this particular item.

Another student of mine passed along this reference question that she had been unable to answer for a patron. The patron had the Hebrew date of the first Hanukah, and wanted to know what the date in the Julian calendar was. The librarian had searched in vain on keywords like "hanukah," "first," "julian," and "date." I took a step back from the question and tried to find the larger subject. I determined that the fact that this date was the first Hanukah was completely irrelevant to the question. The patron had a date in one calendar and needed it "converted" to another. I went to CalendarZone and found a site that converted dates from one calendar to another. We entered the Hebrew date and immediately got the answer the patron needed.

Jean Hewlett of North Bay Cooperative Library System shared with me this eBay story and she even took it one step further than I did: "A patron asked us to find directions for a three-dimensional checkers game that she had purchased at a yard sale. This game had been out of print for many years and the company was no longer in business. After spending several hours with various search engines, I went on eBay, located a copy of the same game, purchased it for $5, and sent her a photocopy of the directions. She was delighted. The game is sitting on my closet shelf, if you know anybody who wants one."

Jean also passed along this story: "A couple of years ago, one of our member libraries wanted to purchase current Filipino music. They had catalogs with lists of recordings, but no way to determine which were old standards and which were currently popular. I found the Web site for a radio station in Manila and e-mailed their program director, who was happy to provide us with their top twenty Filipino recordings."

Lastly, Maureen DeLaughter offers this example using a site almost everyone is familiar with: "Patrons come to the desk not sure of a title, not sure of an author, needing a book review, wanting to know what the next title in a series is, and inevitably Amazon.com is a quick way to find the answer, often easier to search than our OPAC, or Books in Print. Yesterday I had a patron ask for a review of John Sandford's *Night Prey*. I found many reviews quickly on Amazon.com."

COMPLEX REFERENCE EXERCISES

Let's try to answer the following complex reference questions. Just as with the ready reference questions, this section will present the answer, the site used to find the answer, the best (most efficient) method for finding that answer, typical pitfalls, and why the Internet was the better method over print. As with the ready reference questions, this information obtained was accurate as of the writing of this book but may have changed since then.

In order to tackle these questions with the alternate strategy I have presented, here is how you should look at both the questions and the resources given. Try to figure out what the subject of the question is. Treat the list of resources in the subject specific sections on pages 110 and 116 as your OPAC and search it for the appropriate site. These sites are also hyperlinked at the book's Web site. Treat the site that you have chosen as your 'shelf.' Search the 'shelf site' for a more specific site that will have the answer you are looking for. This means that for each question you may end up needing to perform two separate online searches.

COMPLEX REFERENCE QUESTIONS

1. What were the significant world events of 1852?
2. Are there any groups that can help me research my Danish ancestors?
3. How do you say *cheetah* in Swahili?
4. Why is the murder of Francis Scott Key's son historically significant?
5. Who holds the record for the most no-hitters?
6. I just bought a small farm. What do I need to know about growing corn?
7. What can a DVD do that videotape can't?
8. What are the ten most common causes of death in the United States?

COMPLEX REFERENCE ANSWERS

1. *What were the significant world events of 1852?*

Answer:
   First use of the word *evolution*, publication of *Uncle Tom's Cabin*, and the Second Burmese War.

Site Used:
   HyperHistory, available at *www.hyperhistory.com/online_n2/History_n2/a.html*

Best Method (see Figure 5–1):
   Select events from the left side of the page. On the right side of the page select *19th century* then *1851–1860*. Read down the column for 1852 in the center of the page.

Figure 5–1: HyperHistory search result

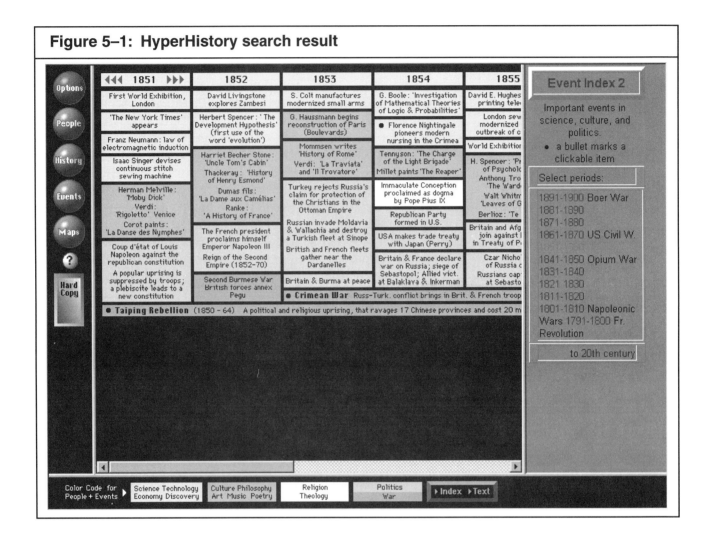

Typical Pitfalls:

The potential overriding problem is this site's use of frames. If you have a low-resolution monitor, the screen will seem crowded. More specifically, many click on the history choice on the left side. This will not get you to the screen of information that you need.

Why the Internet:

This is a case where there is an almost exact print equivalent: *The Timetables of History*. That resource will also give you an answer to this question. For this question the Internet site may be useful if the book is already in use by another patron.

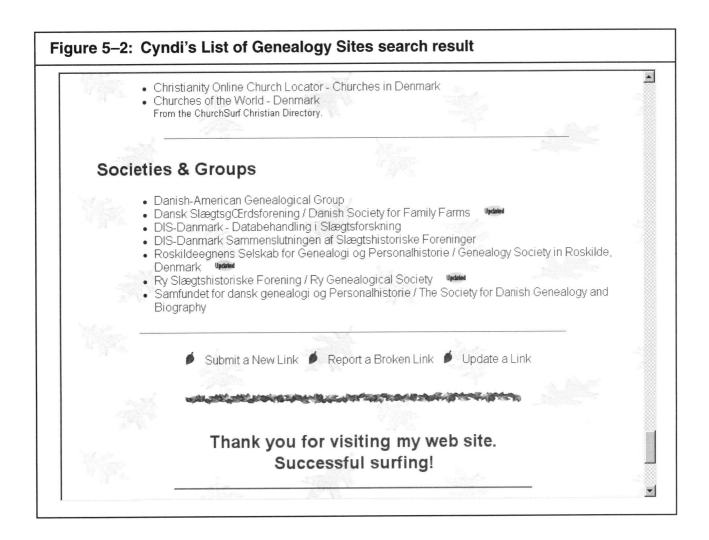

Figure 5–2: Cyndi's List of Genealogy Sites search result

2. *Are there any groups that can help me research my Danish ancestors?*

Answer:
   Yes, the Danish-American Genealogical Group and others.

Site Used:
   Cyndi's List, available at *www.CyndisList.com/*

Best Method (see Figure 5–2):
   Select the Denmark/Danmark link. Scroll down to the Societies & Groups subcategory.

Figure 5–3: The Kamusi Project as found via the Web of Online Dictionaries

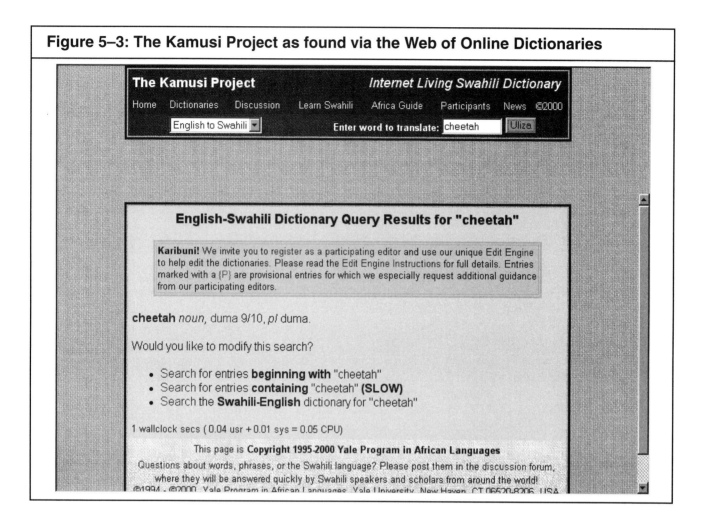

Typical Pitfalls:
This site does have a search function but it is easily overlooked. Also, the sheer number of categories, subcategories, and links in this site can be overwhelming to the novice user.

Why the Internet:
Beyond the print version of this site, there is no single print reference work that I am aware of that non-genealogical libraries would own that could possibly cover the amount of information that this site does.

3. *How do you say* cheetah *in Swahili?*

Answer:
Duma

Site Used:
Web of Online Dictionaries, available at *www.yourdictionary. com/*

Best Method (see Figure 5–3):
Select the *200 more!* link in the page's left column. Select *Swahili* from the list of languages. Pick one of the listed dictionaries, and use that site to find the translation.

Typical Pitfalls:
For this question you are using a directory that will get you to other sites on the relevant subject, in this case English to Swahili dictionaries. The significant problem is that only one of the listed sites for Swahili translates the word in question. At the time of this writing, the one with the answer is the third out of the four sites listed.

Why the Internet:
Many libraries do not have an English-Swahili dictionary in their collection. If your library does not, the Internet is your only other option.

4.   *Why is the murder of Francis Scott Key's son historically significant?*

Answer:
Barton Key was murdered by a U.S. congressman who successfully used the temporary insanity defense for the first time.

Site Used:
HistoryNet, available at *www.thehistorynet.com/*

Best Method (see Figure 5–4):
Click on the site search link. Search on the keywords *francis scott key son murder*. Select the first result.

Typical Pitfalls
Many people when looking for the answer to this question have trouble finding the grey site search button on the site's homepage. Also, from the results that are retrieved, as they are listed, it may not be clear which documents might include the answer In this case, the first one does have the answer, saving the user from needing to read multiple documents in order to find the answer.

Figure 5–4: HistoryNet search result

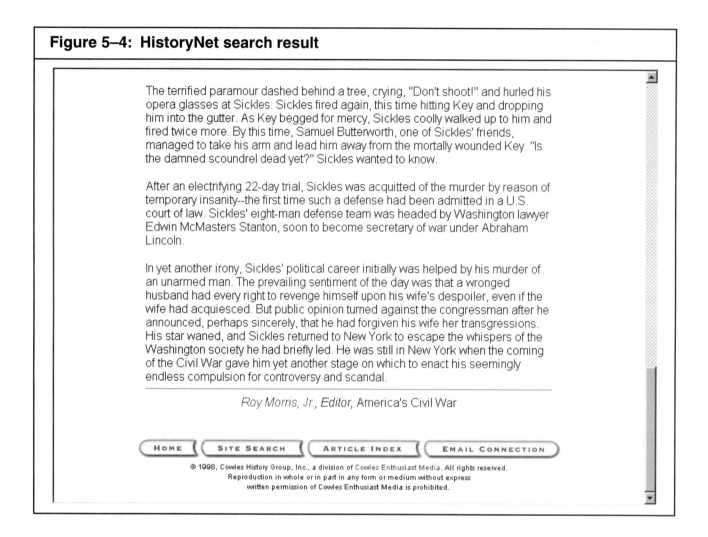

The terrified paramour dashed behind a tree, crying, "Don't shoot!" and hurled his opera glasses at Sickles. Sickles fired again, this time hitting Key and dropping him into the gutter. As Key begged for mercy, Sickles coolly walked up to him and fired twice more. By this time, Samuel Butterworth, one of Sickles' friends, managed to take his arm and lead him away from the mortally wounded Key. "Is the damned scoundrel dead yet?" Sickles wanted to know.

After an electrifying 22-day trial, Sickles was acquitted of the murder by reason of temporary insanity--the first time such a defense had been admitted in a U.S. court of law. Sickles' eight-man defense team was headed by Washington lawyer Edwin McMasters Stanton, soon to become secretary of war under Abraham Lincoln.

In yet another irony, Sickles' political career initially was helped by his murder of an unarmed man. The prevailing sentiment of the day was that a wronged husband had every right to revenge himself upon his wife's despoiler, even if the wife had acquiesced. But public opinion turned against the congressman after he announced, perhaps sincerely, that he had forgiven his wife her transgressions. His star waned, and Sickles returned to New York to escape the whispers of the Washington society he had briefly led. He was still in New York when the coming of the Civil War gave him yet another stage on which to enact his seemingly endless compulsion for controversy and scandal.

Roy Morris, Jr., Editor, America's Civil War

HOME | SITE SEARCH | ARTICLE INDEX | EMAIL CONNECTION

Why the Internet:

Without knowledge of Francis Scott Key's son's name or the name of the murderer, there is little possibility of looking him up in a print resource. A print resource may mention the story under Francis Scott Key, but his more significant contribution to American history, the writing of the national anthem, tends to overshadow this historical footnote. A Web site dedicated to American history is more searchable with the keywords we have and would tend to include more obscure bits of information such as this.

5. *Who holds the record for the most no-hitters?*

Answer:
Nolan Ryan

Figure 5–5: The Baseball Almanac search result as found via SearchSport

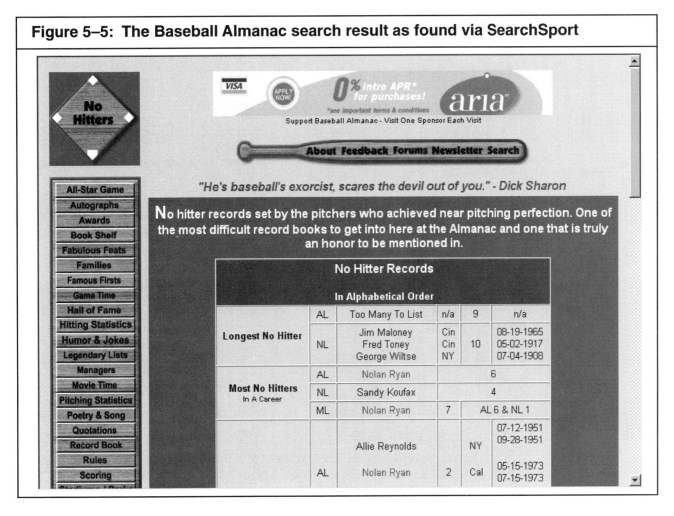

Site Used:
   SearchSport, available at *www.oldsport.com/searchsport/*

Best Method (see Figure 5–5):
   Select the *Baseball* category. Scroll to the bottom of the page and search for *baseball records*. Select the *Baseball Almanac* link. Select *Record Book* from the menu on the left. Scroll down *Pitching Records* and select the link for *Player* in the *No Hitters* category.

Typical Pitfalls:
   Two key pieces of information are needed to answer this question successfully: first, that the sport is baseball and second, that this specifically is a record for pitchers. If you did not know this, a brief reference interview of the patron should get you this information. On the SearchSport site the search function is not ap-

parent. One would expect the search function to be available on the site's homepage but instead the user must first pick a sport and then find the search box at the bottom of a potentially long document.

Why the Internet:
In this case, the Internet may just be faster than finding a sports almanac in your collection (that is, if you have a sports almanac and it is not already being used by another patron or fellow staff member).

6. *I just bought a small farm. What information do I need to know about growing corn?*

Answer:
The Corn Grower's Guidebook, available at *www.kingcorn.org*

Site Used:
AgNIC

Best Method (see Figure 5–6):
Search on the keyword *corn*. The first link is the one mentioned above.

Typical Pitfalls:
The name of the site is not exactly clear. Making the connection between "Ag" and "agriculture" is necessary. Some people also overthink the keywords necessary for the search. Since you are not looking for anything too specific, just the single search term will find what you need.

Why the Internet:
Unless you are in an area known for its agriculture, and more specifically for its corn production, your library will probably not have material on the subject. If it does, the material will probably not go into the detail that the patron needs. The Internet fills in this gap in your print collection.

7. *What can a DVD do that videotape can't?*

Answer:
DVDs provide better sound options, chapter indices, different picture formats, and extra subtitles and/or languages.

Figure 5–6: The KingCorn.com site found via AgNIC

Site Used:
   How Stuff Works, available at *www.howstuffworks.com/*

Best Method (see Figure 5–7):
   Search on *dvd* and select the result titled *How DVDs and DVD Players Work*. From that page select the *What Can They Do* link at the bottom of the page.

Typical Pitfalls:
   The most common problem this question encounters is the overthinking of the keywords that are necessary (as with the "corn" question). In this case just the keyword *dvd* is necessary to get you to the needed information.

Figure 5–7: How Stuff Works search result

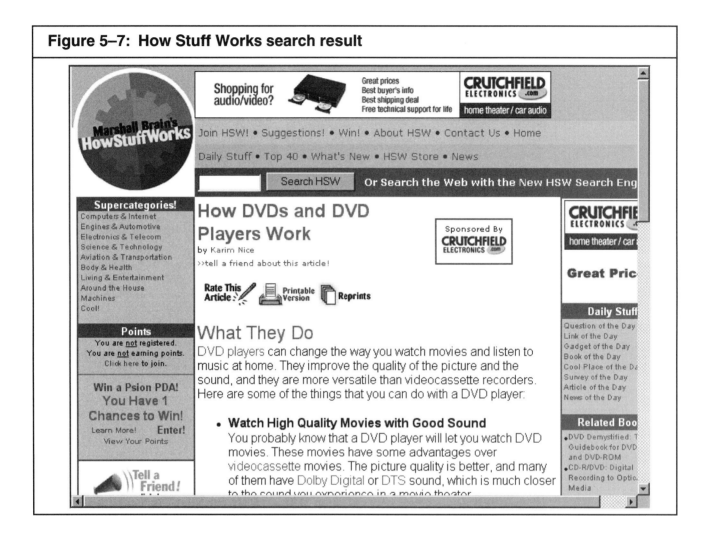

Why the Internet:

Because DVD technology is still relatively new, many collections do not have material on this subject. Those print resources that do exist tend to be more technical in nature; they would give the answer but in much more detail than the patron needs.

8. *What are the ten most common causes of death in the United States?*

Answer:

In order from 1998: heart disease, cancer, stroke, chronic obstructive pulmonary disease, accidents, pneumonia/influenza, diabetes, suicide, nephritis, chronic liver disease.

Figure 5–8: NCHS FastStats search result

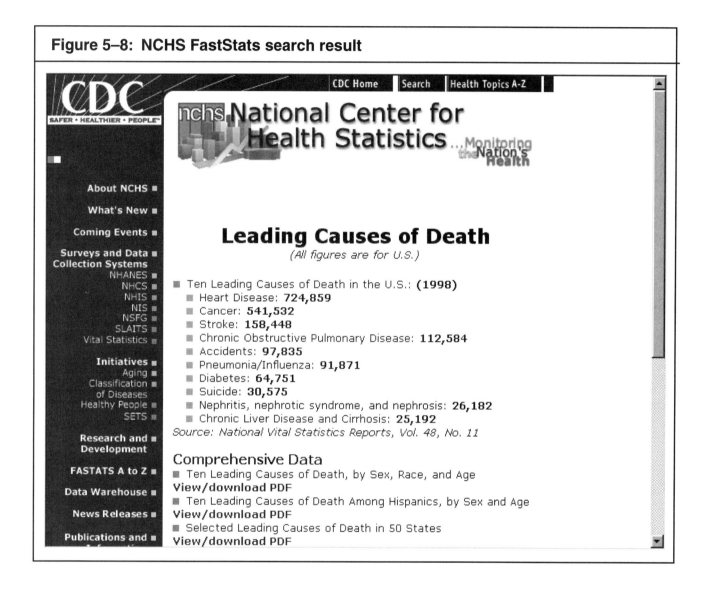

Site Used:
NCHS FastStats, available at *www.cdc.gov/nchs/fastats/*

Best Method (see Figure 5–8):
Scroll down to "leading causes of death" and select that link.

Typical Pitfalls:
In this case, searching the site may be a mistake. The search will find the complete statistical documents in PDF format. In most cases, this will be more information than needed, especially for this question.

Why the Internet:
The site provides quick access to the most common statistics requested. A print resource may go into much more detail than the patron needs, making it more difficult to find the specific answer needed.

I hope these exercises demonstrated the usefulness of the Internet when answering complex reference questions. Learning about these sites and making them part of your reference strategy will build you proficiency and competence using the Internet.

COMPLEX REFERENCE SEARCH ENGINE RESOURCES

GENERAL

AltaVista (*www.altavista.com/*)
AOL NetFind (*http://search.aol.com/*)
Excite (*www.excite.com/*)
Go (*www.go.com/*)
Google (*www.google.com/*)
HotBot (*http://hotbot.lycos.com/*)
LookSmart (*www.looksmart.com/*)
Lycos (*www.lycos.com/*)
Northern Light (*www.northernlight.com/*)
WebCrawler (*www.webcrawler.com/*)

SUBJECT SPECIFIC

Agriculture Network Information Center (*www.agnic.org/*)
"AgNIC is a guide to quality agricultural information on the Internet as selected by the National Agricultural Library, Land-Grant Universities, and other institutions."

AJR NewsLink (*www.newslink.org/searchn.html*)
Sponsored by the American Journalism Review, this site provides search interfaces for AJR articles, their NewsBank, and other news sites.

Argos: Ancient and Medieval Internet (*http://argos.evansville.edu/*)
"Argos is the first peer-reviewed, limited area search engine (LASE) on the World-Wide Web. It has been designed to cover the ancient and medieval worlds. Quality is controlled by a system of hyperlinked internet indices which are managed by qualified professionals who serve as the Associate Editors of the project. The same procedures that govern quality also serve to limit the scope of Argos to the ancient world."

Bartleby.com: Great Books Online (*www.bartleby.com/*)
Links to many resources and searchable databases in the categories of reference, verse, fiction, and nonfiction.

BIRD-ONLINE UK and Irish Business Information Search Engine (*www.bird-online.co.uk/libsearch.html*)
"Choosing either the general or industry specific search engine, you can access our database of UK and Irish sites in a particular category, and/or enter keywords."

BUBL Information Service (*http://bubl.ac.uk/*)
"BUBL is a national information service for the higher education community, funded by JISC, the Joint Information Systems Committee of the Higher Education Funding Councils of England, Scotland and Wales and the Department of Education for Northern Ireland."

Clip Art Searcher (*www.webplaces.com/search/index.htm*)
This site contains several "search forms optimized to find graphics files."

CMU English Server (*http://english-www.hss.cmu.edu/*)
An online collection of over 30,000 electronic publications.

Company Sleuth (*www.companysleuth.com/*)
Company Sleuth is site for the "inside scoop on your favorite companies," it "scours the Internet to bring you the latest information that you can't find anywhere else," and allows you to "get stock quotes, news, insider trades, domain, trademarks and patent registrations and message boards."

DefenseLink (*www.defenselink.mil/*)
This is the Web site for the U.S. Department of Defense. Though not specifically a search engine itself, it does contain a site search engine on the front page that will search a database of more than 22,000 military documents and photos.

Disinformation (*www.disinfo.com/*)
"Disinformation was designed to be the search service of choice for individuals looking for information on current affairs, politics, new science and the 'hidden information,' that seldom seems to slip through the cracks of the corporate-owned media conglomerates."

The Dismal Scientist (*www.dismal.com/economy/releases/new_home.asp*)
"The Dismal Scientist is the web's leading provider of economic analysis. The Dismal Scientist® offers comprehensive and timely economic analysis, tools, message boards, and other features designed to keep our readers fully informed on the state of the world economy."

Ditto (*www.ditto.com/default.asp*)
Search the Web for images based on your keywords. Though this site does find images on almost any topic, the majority of images are copyrighted and permission should be obtained before using any of the found images.

Drink Search (*http://psp.pair.com/cgi-bin/drinksearch.cgi*)
The most complete online resources for mixed drinks. Complete instructions on how to make each drink are included.

Eric's Treasure Troves of Science (*www.astro.virginia.edu/~eww6n/*)
"Here, you will find the extensive on-line encyclopedias of math and science compiled by web encyclopedist Eric W. Weisstein."

Ethnologue: Languages of the World (*www.sil.org/ethnologue/*)
This site includes "164 language maps, 345 overviews of language situations by country, 851 bibliographic references, 6,809 language descriptions, Language name index: 41,000+ alternate names and dialect names and 109 language family trees."

Europages (*www.europages.com/*)
A searchable database of more than half a million companies in 30 European countries. Users can search for information by product/service or company name. A browsable directory is also available.

FindArticles.com (*www.findarticles.com/PI/index.html*)
"FindArticles.com is a vast archive of published articles. Constantly updated, it contains articles dating back to 1998 from more than 300 magazines and journals."

Global Education Locator (*http://nces.ed.gov/globallocator/*)
"Conduct a quick national search and locate information within one of four areas: postsecondary institutions, public schools or districts, public libraries, or private schools in the United States. Or visit the individual sites to conduct more comprehensive searches."

GovBot (*http://ciir2.cs.umass.edu/Govbot/*)
The CIIR GovBot indexes more than 1.5 million Web pages from U.S. government and military sites around the country.

HIPPIAS: Philosophy on the Internet (*http://hippias.evansville.edu/*)
"Hippias is a peer-reviewed search engine that provides access to philosophy-related resources on the World-Wide Web. Quality is controlled by a system of hyperlinked Internet sites which are managed by qualified professionals who serve as the associate editors of the project. The same procedures that govern quality also serve to limit the scope of Hippias to resources of interest to philosophers."

History Net (*www.thehistorynet.com/*)
An online guide to all things historical. The majority of the information provided is from articles unique to this site and the parent company's print magazines and journals.

Human Rights Meta Search Engine (*www1.umn.edu/humanrts/lawform.html*)
A meta search engine designed for easy access to sites dealing with human rights issues. Linked sites include the United Nations, the European Court of Human Rights, Human Rights Watch, and others.

The James Kirk Search Engine (*www.webwombat.com.au/trek/*)
An Australian site dedicated to indexing only sites dealing with the TV series *Star Trek*.

LANDINGS: The Busiest Aviation CyberHub (*www.landings.com/*)
An online guide to all things related to aviation containing more than 100 different categories.

Medieval Feminist Index (*www.haverford.edu/library/reference/mschaus/mfi/mfi.html*)
"The Medieval Feminist Index covers journal articles, book reviews, and essays in books about women, sexuality, and gender during the Middle Ages."

Search.Internet.com (*www.netsearcher.com/*)
Have a question about the Internet or related technologies? Start here, the search engine that only indexes information on those topics.

SearchEdu.com (www.searchedu.com/)
"Over 20 million university and education pages indexed and ranked in order of popularity."

SearchUK (*http://uk.searchengine.com/*)
Indexes only Web sites based in the United Kingdom. A browsable subject directory is also available.

SEC's EDGAR Database (*www.sec.gov/edgarhp.htm*)
Database of corporate information from the U.S. Securities and Exchange Commission.

The Thomas Register of American Manufacturers (*www.thomasregister.com/*)
The Thomas Register contains more than 156,000 American and Canadian companies and more than 135,000 brand names. A free membership is required to use the site.

UNCAT (*www.sapphirepress.com/UNCAT/*)
"UNCAT is the catalog of UNCATaloged titles not generally available in a bookstore or library."

United States Patent and Trademark Office (*www.uspto.gov/patft/index.html*)
Contains the "Full text of all U.S. patents issued since January 1, 1976, and full-page images of each page of every U.S. patent issued since 1790."

Urban Myths.com (*www.urbanmyths.com/*)
Not sure if that story your patron's friend's uncle told her is true or not? Check here for the answer.

U.S. News Archives on the Web (*http://metalab.unc.edu/slanews/internet/archives.html*)
The archive provides the dates of the archive, along with the cost to retrieve the full text of articles for newspapers from all over the United States. Unless noted, searching is free. Charges may apply to retrieve stories. Archives of non-U.S. newspaper archives are also available.

World Biographical Index (*www.biblio.tu-bs.de/acwww25u/wbi_en/*)
"This database is based on the 7th CD-ROM edition of the World Biographical Index containing 2.8 million short biographical entries for eminent individuals who lived in North and South America, Western and Central Europe, Africa, Australia, New Zealand, and Oceania. This edition is also a compiled index to many biographical archives."

World Wide Arts Resources (*http://wwar.com/*)
"This interactive arts gateway will give you access to artists, museums, galleries, high quality art, art history, arts education, antiques, dance, theater, classified ads, resume postings, arts chats, discussion forums and much more."

xrefer (*http://w1.xrefer.com/*)
"Free access to over 450,000 entries—facts, words, concepts, people & quotations covering art, music, history, business, law, literature, health, science and more. xrefer contains encyclopedias, dictionaries, thesauri & books of quotations from the world's leading publishers. All cross-referenced, all in one place—providing you with a single source for reliable factual information."

META

All4One (*www.all4one.com/*)
"Search 4 Popular Specialized Topical Search Engines Simultaneously."

Ask Jeeves (*www.ask.com/*)
"Simply put, Ask Jeeves makes it easy to find answers on the Internet. Enter your question in plain English into the text box on the homepage, then click on the 'Ask' button. Jeeves responds by presenting you with one or more closely related questions to which he knows the answer. Some questions may contain drop-down menus, allowing you to choose from different options."

Copernic (*www.copernic.com/*)
A program that must be downloaded and installed on your PC (not run from a Web site like the other examples), Copernic allows you to simultaneously consult the best search engines, retrieve relevant results with summaries, and automatically remove duplicate information and dead links.

Highway 61 (*www.highway61.com/*)
One of the smaller meta search engines, Highway 61 sends your keywords to Yahoo, Lycos, Webcrawler, Infoseek and Excite.

Mamma (*www.mamma.com/*)
"Mamma.com is a 'Smart Meta Search Engine.' When the user enters a query at the Mamma.com website, Mamma simultaneously queries 10 of the major Search Engines and properly formats the words and syntax for each source being probed. Mamma then creates a virtual database, organizes the results into a uniform format and presents them by relevance and source."

OneSearch (*www.onesearch.com/*)
"OneSearch.com was created in response to the growing need for a new search engine that would cater to the small business person, provide a one-stop-shopping web site with attractive and useful features. We designed and developed OneSearch.com to be capable of providing a meta search function along with keyword bidding, and an easy user interface with all the products and services of the big search engines."

ProFusion (*www.profusion.com/*)
A very fast meta search engine that allows you to choose the resources that your keywords are sent to and allows you to focus better your results based on the topic of your question. The TrackIt service allows you to set up ProFusion to check sites for you and send you an e-mail when they change.

DIRECTORY RESOURCES

GENERAL

About.com (*www.about.com/*)
Takes general directories one step further by having subject-expert volunteers control the listings in each of thousands of categories. This allows those who know the material to decide what should be presented to the site's users.

CyberDewey (*http://ivory.lm.com/~mundie/CyberDewey/CyberDewey.html*)
Sites on many topics organized by Dewey Decimal Number. Although this

site does contain significant gaps it does represent a very interesting way of organizing links.

Finding Data on the Internet: A Journalist's Guide (*http://nilesonline.com/datA*)
Sites organized by a variety of topics; for each topic a particular few sites are recommended. Designed for those without much Internet experience and looking for factual information.

Resource Discovery Network (*www.rdn.ac.uk/*)
"The RDN provides access to a series of Internet resource catalogues containing descriptions of high quality Internet sites, selected and described by specialists from within UK academia and affiliated organisations. Value-added services such as interactive web tutorials and alerting services are also provided to enable users to make more of their time on the Internet."

Yahoo! (*www.yahoo.com*)
The grandfather of all Internet directories. An easy-to-navigate interface allows users to find sites on the topic they are researching.

SUBJECT SPECIFIC

AllReaders.com (*www.allreaders.com/*)
A book review site that let's you choose from hundreds of plot, theme, character, and setting options to find precisely what you'd like to read.

The Animal Omnibus (*www.birminghamzoo.com/ao/*)
"The Animal Omnibus is a list of web sources indexed by the name of the animal. For example, looking up African Elephant will produce a list of hyperlinks to sources with elephant information."

Author Bibliographies (*www.myunicorn.com/biblios.html*)
This site contains bibliographies for more than 5,000 authors. Though not all are complete this is the single largest collection of such lists.

Author Websites (*www.bookwire.com/index/Author-Websites.html*)
An alphabetical listing of official Web sites for hundreds of major authors.

Beaucoup (*www.beaucoup.com/*)
Beaucoup is a categorized directory of subject specific search engines and directories. If I've missed a topic you're looking for in this listing check this site; you'll find one that fits your purposes.

CalendarZone (*www.calendarzone.com/*)
"Comprehensive categorized calendar catalog currently containing countless correlating connections & calzone recipes!"

Cyndi's List of Genealogy Sites on the Internet (*www.CyndisList.com/*)
The most comprehensive genealogy resource on the Web, it contains more than 85,000 links in over 140 categories.

Dead People Server (*http://dpsinfo.com/*)
"Remember whats'er name? She played the girl in that dumb movie with whoziss. What ever happened to her? Specifically, is she dead yet? Here's where to find out. The Dead People Server is simply a list of interesting celebrities who are long dead, newly dead or might plausibly be dead. They may be 'retired' or spaced. DPS tells you who has really Rung Down the Curtain and Joined the Choir Invisible, and who's Just Resting. To help the terminally confused, I've been building a Quash Those Death Rumors page."

Descriptions of Non-Christian Faith Groups and Ethical Systems (*www.religioustolerance.org/var_rel.htm*)
"We categorize groups according to how they themselves regard their beliefs. Some are listed in more than one section, because their memberships are divided on whether they should be considered Christian or not. Information for these essays was extracted from reliable sources, and believed to be accurate and reasonably unbiased. Where possible, they have been reviewed by a group (typically 3) of persons who follow the belief." The site also contains similar information on "Christian faith groups" and cults.

Directory of Scholarly and Professional E-Conferences (*www.mailbase.ac.uk/kovacs/*)
"The Directory of Scholarly and Professional E-conferences screens, evaluates and organizes discussion lists, newsgroups, MUDS, MOO'S, Muck's, Mushes, mailing lists, interactive Web chat groups etc. (e-conferences) on topics of interest to scholars and professionals for use in their scholarly, pedagological and professional activities."

EuroSeek (*www.euroseek.net/*)
A directory of Internet resources divided into subject categories. Designed specifically for the European community and available in more than 40 languages.

FindLaw (*www.findlaw.com/*)
Similar to Yahoo!, but this directory is only for legal resources.

4000 Years of Women in Science (*www.astr.ua.edu/4000WS/4000WS.html*)
"This site lists over 125 names from our scientific and technical past. They are all women! This site grew out of the public talks given by Dr. Sethanne Howard, currently with the National Science Foundation. We hope you will share what you know with us. This includes inventors, scholars and writers as well as mathematicians and astronomers."

Hardin Meta Directory of Internet Health Resources (*www.lib.uiowa.edu/hardin/md/*)
This directory lists other medical guides in more than 40 categories. Each category is broken down into large lists, medium lists, and small lists.

How Stuff Works (*www.howstuffworks.com/*)
"Have you ever wondered how the engine in your car works or what makes your refrigerator cold? Then How Stuff Works is the place for you! Click on the categories below to see hundreds of cool articles."

HyperHistory (*www.hyperhistory.com/online_n2/History_n2/a.html*)
Set up like *The Timetables of History* book, HyperHistory contains more than "2,000 files covering 3,000 years of world history."

Knowledge Hound: The 'How-To' Hunter (*www.knowledgehound.com/*)
"Knowledge Hound is the Web's biggest directory of free how-tos and your fastest way to hunt a how-to down. From sports to hobbies to computers and much, much more."

National Geographic Xpeditions (*www.nationalgeographic.com/xpeditions/main.html*)
"You've got the whole world in your hands—and nearly 600 National Geographic maps at your fingertips. Just click to a state, province, country, or continent; choose your settings; and print away! (Crisp and clear, these page-size maps were designed for printing and copying.) Or grab a map to share online."

NCHS FastStats A to Z (*www.cdc.gov/nchs/fastats/*)
An alphabetical listing of statistics on hundreds of topics from the (U.S.) National Center for Health Statistics.

The Science Fiction Resource Guide (*http://sflovers.rutgers.edu/WeB/SFRG/*)
The most complete independent guide to science fiction resources on the Internet. Hosted by Rutgers University.

Search Sport (*www.oldsport.com/searchsport/index.html*)
Categorized listings of over 7,000 sports-related sites.

The Smoking Gun (*www.thesmokinggun.com/*)
"The Smoking Gun brings you exclusive documents—cool, confidential, quirky—that can't be found elsewhere on the Web. Using material obtained from government and law enforcement sources, via Freedom of Information requests, and from court files nationwide, we guarantee everything here is 100% authentic."

Statistical Resources on the Web (*www.lib.umich.edu/libhome/Documents.center/stats.html*)
From the University of Michigan Documents Center, this site categorizes thousands of links to sites with statistics on topics ranging from agriculture to weather.

Telephone Directories on the Web (*www.contractjobs.com/tel/*)
"This is the Internet's original and most complete index of online phone books, with over 400 links to Yellow Pages, White Pages, Business Directories, Email Addresses and Fax Listings from over 170 countries all around the world."

Web Elements (*www.shef.ac.uk/chemistry/web-elements/*)
A complete online periodic table of elements with all you need to know about each element. Be sure to check out the cartoons associated with each element.

Web of Online Dictionaries (*www.yourdictionary.com/*)
This site has a quick English dictionary and thesaurus lookup along with a directory of links to online dictionaries of more than 240 languages.

WebCam Central (*www.camcentral.com/*)
Your online guide to live Web-cams.

WebMolecules (*www.webmolecules.com/index.html*)
Contains more than 22,000 3-D molecular models viewable by category or formula.

The WWW Library Directory (*www.webpan.com/msauers/libdir/*)
A geographically organized directory of more than 7,000 library Web sites in more than 130 countries.

WWWomen (*www.wwwomen.com/*)
"Launched in 1996, WWWomen.com screens every link submission for relevancy to women's interests. We don't try to list every link and give you a lot of irrelevant search results—we try to list the quality links you want to surf for. And because we screen links, we don't include adult and offensive links. Even given this stringent review, WWWomen still offers the largest collection of exclusively female-oriented web links online."

REVIEWED

AlphaSearch (*www.calvin.edu/library/searreso/internet/as/*)
"The primary purpose of AlphaSearch is to access the finest Internet 'gateway' sites. The authors of these 'gateway' sites have spent significant time gathering into one place all relevant sites related to a discipline, subject, or idea. You have instant access to hundreds of sites by entering just one gateway site. You reap what others have sown and nurtured!"

Argus Clearinghouse (*www.clearinghouse.net/*)
"The Argus Clearinghouse provides a central access point for value-added topical guides which identify, describe, and evaluate Internet-based information resources." Sites are rated on the following categories: Resource Description, Resource Evaluation, Guide Design, Organization Schemes, and Guide Meta-information.

Britannica.com (*www.britannica.com/*)
Sites are described and rated on the following scale: Noteworthy, Recommended, Excellent, Superior, and Best of the Web.

The Scout Report (*scout.cs.wisc.edu*)
Sponsored by the Internet Scout Project, the Scout Report is a biweekly newsletter of new and noteworthy sites. The Web site allows you to search its archive of over 10,500 reviews sites.

UniGuide Academic Guide to the Internet (*www.aldea.com/guides/ag/attframes2.html*)
"The UniGuide Academic Guide to the Internet is the Internet guide created especially for the higher education community. Its goal is to develop the primary Internet resource of and for the research and academic community. Each site selected for inclusion in the UniGuide Academic Guide to the Internet has been reviewed for appropriateness by a staff of librarians and content experts. The topical listings of the UniGuide Academic Guide to the Internet focus exclusively on the interests of the higher education research and education communities. The top level categories are primarily science oriented and include Biological Sciences, Computer & Info Sciences, Education & Human Sciences, Engineering, Geosciences, Mathematical & Physical Sciences, Social, Behavioral & Economic Sciences and Liberal Arts."

6 EXPLORING LARGER ISSUES OF INTERNET REFERENCE

SURVEYING PROFESSIONAL EXPERIENCES OF E-MAIL REFERENCE

I will briefly touch on a slightly different angle of our subject. We have looked at the librarian using the Internet to find the answers; now we will look at the patron using the Internet to pose the questions.

Many libraries are now starting to think outside the box when it comes to offering more direct reference service to patrons who are not on the premises. Most libraries have been taking reference questions over the phone for decades and some even via the fax for years. More recently some libraries are offering reference services via e-mail.

Bernie Sloan's guide to e-mail reference sites (*www.lis.uiuc.edu/~b-sloan/e-mail.html*) is a great place to find many examples of libraries offering this type of service. From his page you have direct access to the Web pages of more than 90 libraries in which this service is offered. If you are considering e-mail reference, you can find many great examples there.

Now the question becomes whether offering this service is worth the time and effort put into it. I wondered just how successful it has been for the libraries that are offering it.

I wanted to conduct an informal survey to try and gauge the success of libraries offering reference services via the Internet. I posted this question to several statewide electronic mailing lists for librarians and Web4Lib, an electronic mailing list for libraries offering Internet access to their patrons. I asked what type of library they were, how long they had been offering the service, and whether they found it successful.

Most also told me what effect reference service via e-mail was

---

> One library, Virginia Tech, responded that they had just started a chat-based reference service. This service can be found at *www.lib.vt.edu/research/liveref.html*.

having on their staff. The effect was generally minimal because very few of their patrons used the service. All of the libraries that responded indicated that the service, whether at a college, university, or public library, was underutilized.

It is difficult to draw any concrete conclusions about this area. Here is a sample of the interesting responses I received:

> We have offered e-mail reference service only since the beginning of [2000]. We have had, to my knowledge, 4 takers. That is, in spite of links prominently placed on our web pages, and in spite of mentioning the service to all the freshmen at Orientation and to every B.I. class this year, we have received exactly 4 reference questions by e-mail in about 2 months of offering it. That is less than I'd hoped, more than I'd feared, and actually about what I would expect for a new service and at the beginning of the year. (Julia Schult, Elmira College, NY)

> We have been offering the service since 1998, with [a Web page]. It certainly doesn't get an overwhelming number of questions (1-2/week), but we still consider it successful as supplying another route for patrons to interact with the library. (Eric Robbins, Northbrook Public Library, IL)

> The Central Aurora Public Library does have email access for customers to ask questions, however, we have had it for a very short time. So far, we have had no takers, but are in the process of doing some publicity. (Kathy Lawrence, Aurora Public Library, CO)

> I don't consider it that big a success because the usage is very light—maybe a couple of questions a month. There is really no way to filter questions from outside our geographic area either. (Robert VanderHart, The Lamar Souter Library, Worcester, MA)

> We just started offering this service when our homepage was updated in August [of 2000]. We have averaged about one question per week. (Sybil Barnes, Estes Park Public Library, CO)

> We have answered about 60 questions since April 19, 2000. (Jill Stockinger, Sacramento Public Library, CA)

It went live during the summer of 1998. We average about 2 questions a month, mostly from people not affiliated with the university. We still try to answer those questions, since they do not take up a large amount of time and occasionally, they do deal with Evansville or the university. (Margaret Atwater-Singer, University of Evansville, KY)

Despite the majority of responses to my request indicating that the use of the service was underwhelming, there were several people who did indicate the service was a success. Here are three of the responses that gave the strongest indication of success. Interestingly, two of three are from Canada.

We do it here. Each unit that offers e-mail reference has their own policies and procedures. I handle it for Government Documents and for Maps. We probably get 150-200 a year for GovDocs and 50 for Maps. (Kendall Simmons, University of Kansas)

We've had our e-mail reference for 2 years now. We consider it wildly successful. We have never advertised it but are now averaging 2–3 questions a day with some days up to 11. We've gotten questions from Singapore, New Zealand, Australia, Spain, France, Britain, a few countries in South America, all over Canada and all over the United States. (Mark Roesner, Edmonton Public Library, Alberta, Canada)

The children's section of Ask Us began in September 1997. The service was not advertised and got off to a slow start but has grown steadily. When amalgamation created the new Toronto Public Library, the staff of the Albion Branch in the West Region continued to answer the questions directed to the children's section of Ask Us, while the Answerline staff at the Toronto Reference Library answered those questions directed to the adult section. The number of questions increased by 35% between the first six months of 1998 and the first six months of 1999. We have experienced a further increase of 42% in the first six months of 2000. So far in 2000, we have answered 658 questions. Questions come from all over the world: various parts of Canada and the U.S., Turkey, France, England, Russia, Korea, Mexico. Most questions, of course, come from Toronto. Questions fall into four categories: titles, library services, curriculum driven subjects, and subjects of personal interest. Consistently, most questions are for information about library services and information to complete a school assignment. Because this is a "quick answer" service, we tend to point people to places where they can find answers as opposed to giving answers, but we have occasionally spent a lot of time finding the answer to a question. We get surprisingly little "junk mail," only a few answers have been returned to us because the address was no good, and we've even received a few thank yous. We consider it a very successful service, judging by the growth. (Linda Deterville, Albion Branch, Toronto Public Library, Canada)

On a more cautionary note, I received the following response from Nancy Bolt, the state librarian of Colorado, which may give a reason for the lack of use of e-mail-based reference service.

Most of the on-line reference services I've seen have something like: Send us your question and we'll check our e-mail a couple of times a day and we promise to get back to you in 24 hours. I think that's terrible. Most people who want an answer, want an answer. They might be willing to wait for extensive research but if I want quick information, I'm going to call, not e-mail. People like the idea of on-line but often it seems the service is worse than telephone service.

INVESTIGATING COMPETITION TO TRADITIONAL LIBRARY REFERENCE

Now let's take a brief look at whether the Internet poses any challenges to traditional reference service. What is the Internet competition to the services offered by individual libraries?

Although the above quote deals with the Internet Public Library which, since it is library-based, I do not view as direct competition to the more traditional library reference, it does make a very good point. For one reason or another, some potential patrons are going to the Internet to find the answers to their questions.

In the past one to two years, a new type of Internet resource

> The Internet Public Library (*www.ipl.org*) was founded in 1995 as part of a class project, wherein library school students and volunteers would provide free online reference services. The patrons of the IPL's reference services may not, in fact, use their local libraries. "Many patrons indicate that they can't get to a library . . . . others clearly don't want to go," and some patrons have "questions too personal to ask in person." Using a computer-mediated method of communication might free some patrons from time and travel constraints, but others will benefit from being spared a sense of shame or embarrassment.
>
> Source: Kenneth R. Irwin. "Professional Reference Service at the Internet Public Library with 'Freebie' Librarians." *Searcher,* October 1, 1998. p. 21.

has appeared. Known as "Ask-a..." sites, these sites link people with questions to people that have answers.

One of these sites is All Experts. This site breaks down into categories. A person goes to the site with a question and picks the appropriate category. In the category is a listing of volunteer experts on that topic. The person reads brief descriptions of the available volunteers and checks the feedback that volunteer has received from previous questioners.

The user picks a volunteer that they feel they can trust to give a correct answer and fills out a form with their question. The volunteer then receives an e-mail notifying them of the question. The volunteer can then decide to answer the question or not. Providing an answer is sent back to the user, the user can then rate the volunteer on such items as politeness, timeliness, and accuracy of the answer.

I wrote to the owner of the All Experts site, Steven J. Gordon. When asked what he felt the difference between his service and library reference he replied: "Reference desks point people to books, or look up things in books. Our service is less focused on giving facts, then giving how-to advice—how to fix your car, or how to deal with your pet, or what to see in Mexico, etc."

When I posted the question of this type of site creating competition to librarians most library staff did not seem very worried about these services or even thought to consider them as "com-

> I use the All Experts as an example here because I am a volunteer on that site in the Web Design and Internet Searching categories.

petition." The first response is from a volunteer for such services who does not view them as competition.

> Even though these sites offer free experts on various topics, I don't really see them as effective competition to reference librarians. These sites are really good at taking advantage of the knowledge dispersed throughout the online community, but they are not so good at finding 10 sources for a research paper due in 2 days... Students want things immediately, full-text, online. Most of them don't even want to walk to a journal and photocopy an article. Many of the sites don't give immediate answers, and students won't want to wait 3 days for an answer. (Wayne Bivens-Tatum, Gettysburg College, PA)

The second respondent is also a volunteer for such services but does view them as competition.

> From my experience, I have come to the conclusion that these services pose a threat to libraries and to the work librarians do, for several reasons. First, the public frequently is satisfied with "good enough" information. Second, many if not most members of the public do not know how to evaluate the quality of the information they are receiving from an Ask-A service. Third, they want the information fast and delivered in a nice neat package. The public does not want to do the work themselves. And fourth they are wanting the information for free or are willing to pay little to nothing for the information. (Monika Antonelli, University of North Texas)

I believe that these sites do not pose an immediate threat to traditional library reference but that threat is on the horizon. I also believe that others in the library community agree with me on this. I recently happened upon the following (paraphrased) ad which may prove this point:

> NOW HIRING LIBRARIANS FOR WEB-BASED REFERENCE SERVICES. Question-and-answer Web site seeks qualified library professionals with both general and specialized knowledge to answer queries posted to our Web site. This isn't a full- or part-time job; simply register on the site and select categories of questions to answer when they come in. Earn supplemental income

by answering questions at your leisure, with no commitment.

If you are interested in trying out any of these services here is a list of the more popular sites that offer question and answer services.

AllExperts   *www.allexperts.com*

WHquestion *www.whquestion.com*

AskMe   *www.askme.com*

WebHelp   *www.webhelp.com/home*

APPENDIX A: READY REFERENCE META PAGES

These sites are set up to be directories of reference resources. Some of them are more ready reference oriented, others more subject oriented. These are all examples of what libraries and other organizations have created to assist them with the new ready reference strategy as discussed in Chapter 3.

ResearchIt! (*www.itools.com/research-it/research-it.html*)
The Internet Public Library (*www.ipl.org/ref/*)
My Virtual Reference Desk (*www.refdesk.com/instant.html*)
Online Reference Desk (*www.sil.org/general/reference.html*)
University of Washington Libraries: Reference Tools
    (*www.lib.washington.edu/research/az.html*)
Coe College Quick Reference Page (*www.public.coe.edu/departments/*
    Library/quickref.html)
Galaxy's EINET Reference (*http://galaxy.tradewave.com/galaxy/*
    Reference.html)
University of Texas at Austin Quick Reference (*www.lib.utexas.edu/Libs/*
    PCL/Reference.html)

APPENDIX B:
ONLINE VERTICAL FILES

The sites in this section are online versions of library or other organizations' collections of unrelated facts and figures. Some of the sites are searchable; others are browsable by subject. What can be found in each of these sites widely varies, as do actual vertical files. I strongly suggest that you take the time to familiarize yourself with these sites before you try to use them in answering live reference questions.

The Fugitive Fact File (*www.hennepin.lib.mn.us/pub/search/fff_public.html*)
"The Fugitive Fact File was compiled by Hennepin County Library staff from information files maintained at individual libraries throughout the Hennepin County Library System. The purpose of this database, which brings information from those many files together into one online resource, is to assist patrons in locating hard-to-find and elusive information. All of the data and resources collected here have been used by library staff to answer reference questions. The Fugitive Fact File is a full text database, therefore all terms which appear in the TITLE, TEXT, and KEYWORDS fields, are fully searchable. KEYWORDS are additional and alternative terms which help link related facts together for enhanced retrieval. In addition, appropriate Web sites have been added to many of the facts in the database and can be accessed easily by clicking on the link."

Ready Reference Files (*www.santacruzpl.org/readyref/*)
"These files contain information on subjects that the reference staff has found tricky to find. They include all kinds of subjects, except for Santa Cruz local history."

Harper's Index (*http://harpers.org/harpers-index/listing.php3*)
This is the online version of the printed index from *Harper's* magazine. The facts and statistics presented change monthly so you never know what you'll find.

NOTES AND CREDITS

Used with permission by Brad Coon
Available at *www.fortunecity.com/rivendell/everquest/624/feorran.html*

2–24 The homepage of Brad's Conlang and Conculture pages
Used with permission by Brad Coon
Available at *www.fortunecity.com/rivendell/everquest/624/index.html*

3–1 The Coe College Quick Reference page
Used with permission by Coe College Library
Available at *www.public.coe.edu/departments/Library/quickref.html*

3–2 The University of Texas at Austin Quick Reference page
Used with permission by the General Libraries, The University of Texas at Austin
Available at *www.lib.utexas.edu/Libs/PCL/Reference.html*

3–3 The University of Washington Reference Tools by Title page
Used with permission by the University of Washington Library
Available at *www.lib.washington.edu/research/az.html*

3–4 The University at Buffalo Reference Sources on the Net page
Used with permission by the University at Buffalo Library
Available at *http://ublib.buffalo.edu/libraries/e-resources/selected.html*

3–5 The University of California at Berkeley Electronic Reference Resources page
Used with permission by University of California at Berkeley Libraries
Available at *http://sunsite.berkeley.edu/cgi-bin/searchref.pl?keyword=&DC.subject=Reference&DC.type&display=brief*

3–6 The University of London Library Rapid Reference page
Used with permission by University of London Library
Available at *www.uul.ac.uk/ull/*

3–7 Rhyme Zone search result
Used with permission by Rhyme Zone
Available at *www.rhymezone.com/r/rhyme.cgi?Word=orange&typeofrhyme=perfect&org1=syl&org2=l*

3–8 Absolute Trivia search result
Used with permission by Absolute Trivia
Available at *www.absolutetrivia.com/search.cgi?query=rhyme+orange*

3–9 Symbols of the World search result
Used with permission by Symbols.com
Available at *www.symbols.com/encyclopedia/20/2023.html*

5–1   HyperHistory search result
      Used with permission by Andreas Nothiger
      Available at *www.hyperhistory.com/*

5–2   Cyndi's List of Genealogy Sites search result
      Used with permission by Cyndi's List of Genealogy Sites
        on the Internet
      Available at *www.cyndislist.com/denmark.htm*

5–3   The Kamusi Project as found via the Web of Online
        Dictionaries
      Used with permission by the Kamusi Project Internet Liv-
        ing Swahili Dictionary
      Available at *www.yale.edu/swahili/*

5–4   HistoryNet search result
      Used with permission by HistoryNet
      Available at *www.thehistorynet.com/AmericasCivilWar/
        editorials/1998/1198.htm*

5–5   The Baseball Almanac search result as found via
        SearchSport
      Used with permission by the Baseball Almanac
      Available at *http://baseball-almanac.com/rb_noh1.shtml*

5–6   The KingCorn.com site found via AgNIC
      Used with permission by KingCorn.com
      Available at *www.kingcorn.com/*

5–7   How Stuff Works search result
      Used with permission by HowStuffWorks.com
      Available at *www.howstuffworks.com.dvd7.htm*

5–8   NCHS FastStats search result
      Available at *www.cdc.gov//nchs/fastats/lcod.htm*

INDEX

E

Eaton (CO) Public Library, 97
eBay, 26, 97–98
Edmonton (Alberta, Canada) Public Library, 123
Elmira (NY) College, 122
E-mail-based reference, xi, 121–124
Encyclopedias, 93
Estes Part (CO) Public **Library, 122**
EuroSearch, 82

F

Favorites. *See* Bookmarks
FindLaw, 80
Finegold, L.X., 30–31
FirstSearch. *See* OCLC
Fleishman, Dorothy, 1
Fortune City, 39
Fundamentally Eccentric Premise, A, 30–34

G

Garwood, Steve, 2
GE. *See* General Electric
General Electric, 97
Gettysburg (PA) College, 126
Google, 79–81, 84–86, 91, 97
Gordon, Stephen J., 125
GovBot, 82

H

Hanukah, 98
Hewlett, Jean, 98
Hit counters, 23–25
Hot AIR. *See* Annals of Improbable Research
HotBot, 19, 79–81, 91
HowStuffWorks.com, 107–108
HTML, 56
Hunberger, Joy, 97
HyperHistory, 85, 99–100

I

Inference Find, 82
Internet, x–xi, 1–2, 11, 18, 47–52, 54–55, 61, 72–73
 benefits over print, 3–4

downsides, 5
evaluating, 7, 11–27, 43–45
exercises, 27–43
filtering, 12
quality, 6
resources, 43–45
size, 6
Internet Dictionary Project, The, 66–67
Internet Explorer, 54
Internet Public Library, The, 125
Irwin, Kenneth R., 125

J

Jackson, WY, 90
Jadad, Alejandro R., 14
JAMA. *See Journal of the American Medical Association,*
James Kirk Search Engine, The, 82
Johns Hopkins Antibiotic Guide, 87–88
Journal of the American Medical Association, 14

K

Kamusi Project, The, 102
Key, Barton, 103–104
Key, Francis Scott, 93, 99, 103–104
KingCorn.com, 106–107

L

Ladies Against Women, 27, 34–36, 43
Lamar Souter Library (Worcster, MA), 122
Lawrence, Kathy, 122
Lexis/Nexis, 11–12
Libraries,
 Aurora (CO) Public, 122
 Birmingham (AL) Public, 1
 Camden (NJ) Public, 2
 Eaton (CO) Public, 97
 Edmonton (Alberta, Canada) Public, 123
 Estes Part (CO) Public, 122
 Internet Public, 125
 Lamar Souter (Worcester MA), 122
 Northbrook (IL) Public, 122
 Sacramento (CA) Public, 122
 Toronto (Canada) Public, 123–124

ABOUT THE AUTHOR

Michael P. Sauers is the Internet Trainer for the Biographical Center for Research's Internet and Database Services programs. Prior to joining BCR in 1997, he was an independent consultant and trainer in Las Vegas, Nevada. He has also worked for both the New York State Library and the New York State Assembly. He earned his MLS from the University of Albany's School of Information Science and Policy, State University of New York, in 1995.

Michael is the author of *Using Microsoft Outlook 2000: A How-To-Do-It Manual for Librarians* (Neal-Schuman, 2001), *Microsoft FrontPage 2000: Advanced Topics* (Quessing Courseware Corporation, 2000), and *The Collector's Guide to Dean Koontz* (Cemetery Dance Publications, 2001).

You can find out more information about Michael's classes, presentations, publications, and other projects at *http://www.bcr.org/ ~msauers/*.